Unsheltered Love

Praise for Unsheltered Love

"With a pandemic raging, our nation's cities under siege and residents sheltered in place, Traci Medford-Rosow and her husband, Joel, see what no one else was looking for—homeless men and women--and take a leap of faith to show the unsheltered love. Daily walks in their neighborhood led them to become involved with new friends that most in their city shunned and even feared. Traci became especially close to a battered and abused homeless woman named Maggie while Joel dreamed of a city where no one goes hungry or sleeps on the streets. Handing out home-made sandwiches to strangers, they did not look away from distress. While nobody can help everybody, they proved that everybody can help somebody. As you turn the pages of this well-written and hopeful story, keep an open mind and eyes for ways to make a difference. *Unsheltered Love* is worthy of your time."

**–Ron Hall, #1 *New York Times* bestselling author
of *Same Kind of Different as Me, Workin' Our Way
Home* and *What Difference do it Make?***

"Medford-Rosow relates the stories of several people in New York City who were homeless at the start of the COVID pandemic. In March 2020, the author and her husband noticed the increased number of unhoused people living on the streets of their New York City neighborhood. Concerned about their survival, Medford-Rosow brought them sandwiches regularly and gradually befriended several. She tells each person's story, focusing on how they came to be homeless and the efforts to find them social services and a room. The stories of the unhoused people are contrasted with events from the author's own life, demonstrating that the circumstances that cause people to lose their homes are not uncommon. At the end of each chapter, Maggie Wright, one of Medford-Rosow's unhoused friends, gives her perspective on the chapter's events, providing additional insight. The author ponders the impact that the first year of the pandemic and New York City's COVID policies had on the unhoused population.

VERDICT: A moving account of the experience of unhoused people in a major American city."

–Library Journal

"Revealing the power of being present and listening to others, Traci Medford-Rosow's memoir Unsheltered Love covers her encounters with people facing homelessness during COVID-19. In the early days of the pandemic, Medford-Rosow and her husband Joel began taking walks to give food and supplies to homeless people near their home in New York City. Along the way, they listened to people's stories and grappled with their own privilege and desire to create lasting change. Across a year and half span, Medford-Rosow shares the stories of those she interacted with, including Maggie Wright, whose clear, honest voice and willingness to share her story is a gift. Her journal entries reveal her pain, hope, how she learned to trust again, and how she began rebuilding all she'd lost. Moved along by engaging conversations that reveal both Medford-Rosow's perspective and the perspectives of Maggie and other homeless people, the book includes insights about life on the streets, where money helps to buy food, but also when it comes to buying a cup of coffee in order to use the bathroom at McDonald's. So, too, are there grueling truths about what it means to try to help, and about how investments of time and money often yield few results. Still, the book is generous with hope—both from Medford-Rosow and from the people she's met. Medford-Rosow is humble in revealing what she had to learn the hard way: the book's late updates on the people covered herein include both positive developments and evidence that not everyone makes it through.

Unsheltered Love is a moving memoir about pandemic connections formed with people facing homelessness."

–Foreword Reviews

"A New Yorker connects with her unhoused neighbors in this memoir. Medford-Rosow's story of developing meaningful personal relationships with houseless people who spent their days near her Manhattan home is effectively a 2020 time capsule. It recounts the changes that Covid-19 brought to New York City and offers a humane account of the realities that people without housing face. The sudden shutdown of many local businesses in March 2020 meant that local panhandlers had few donors, so Medford-Rosow and her husband, Joel, began taking daily walks through their neighborhood, first offering people dollar bills and then homemade sandwiches. Over time, they developed close relationships with several people, got to know their stories, and supported them as they tried to move into sheltered housing. Medford-Rosow connected most deeply with a woman who served as this book's developmental editor and contributed short essays to the text under the pseudonym Maggie Wright; in them, she writes about the same events as the author but from her own perspective. In these pages, Medford-Rosow writes about emotional moments with an admirable lack of sentimentality. Throughout, she takes pains not to portray herself and Joel as heroic— for instance, she still worries that the city's plan to use nearby hotels as shelters will hurt local property values—and she offers no broad policy recommendations. Instead, Maggie's personal journey, with its many setbacks and successes, serves as the book's core, and it's an effective one; her middle-class background and struggles with addiction are likely to resonate with many readers. The book also does an effective job of evoking the uncertainty of the early days of the Covid-19 pandemic, from the initial assumptions that offices would only be closed briefly to phases of reopening to premature claims of victory as the first wave receded.

A focused and engaging remembrance of a specific community changed by the Covid-19 pandemic."

–Kirkus Reviews

"This true story is as hopeful as it is heart-wrenching. It takes place on the fringe of society where most of us dare not look. The author did more than look. Surviving on the streets of New York City is a difficult life, during a pandemic it is a virtual death sentence. Before long, the reader is immersed in an unimaginable world fraught with peril. We meet some of its brave—yes, brave—inhabitants, learn their stories, and see them through the eyes and hearts of the author and her husband. They took a personal interest in each and every one they met and offered something that is in dangerously short supply on the streets. I was so moved by this compelling story of hardship and hope that my heart would not let me put it down."

–David Homick, author of *Broken Angels, Reason to Live*, and *From Time to Time*.

"When Traci and Joel begin handing out sandwiches on the streets of New York City, they are drawn into the lives of nine homeless people. *Unsheltered Love* is a powerful story of how one couple makes a difference during the height of the pandemic. This groundbreaking story, filled with insight and inspiration, gives us a glimpse into the transformation that is possible when people look beyond the face of poverty and desperation into the heart of humanity."

–Ann Campanella, bestselling author of *Motherhood: Lost and Found, Celiac Mom* and *What Flies Away*.

"Like Alice down the Rabbit Hole, *Unsheltered Love* drops us into the surreal world of homelessness, filled with characters no less crazy than the Mad Hatter. Only these characters are real and living on the streets of New York! Author Traci Medford-Rosow shows us all how someone, just like us, a neighbor and a fellow traveler, decided to grab hold of anonymous outstretched hands during this strange pandemic, to provide human connection and support, and eventually, a path upward, out of the rabbit hole of homelessness."

–Linda Heagy, Hand in Hand by Glynn.

"Traci Medford-Rosow dares to get involved with the homeless in New York City during the pandemic. Highly motivating, this book is heart wrenching and necessary to read to understand street plight. A real story about real people. Simply superb."

–Gail Gessert, Ph.D. Educational Psychology.

Unsheltered
LOVE

Homelessness, Hunger, and Hope
in a City under Siege

TRACI MEDFORD-ROSOW

With Journal Excerpts by Maggie Wright

NEW YORK

LONDON • NASHVILLE • MELBOURNE • VANCOUVER

Unsheltered LOVE

Homeslessness, Hunger, and Hope in a City under Siege

Published in New York, New York, by Morgan James Publishing. Morgan James is a trademark of Morgan James, LLC. www.MorganJamesPublishing.com

Proudly distributed by Ingram Publisher Services.

Morgan James BOGO™

A **FREE** ebook edition is available for you or a friend with the purchase of this print book.

CLEARLY SIGN YOUR NAME ABOVE

Instructions to claim your free ebook edition:
1. Visit MorganJamesBOGO.com
2. Sign your name CLEARLY in the space above
3. Complete the form and submit a photo of this entire page
4. You or your friend can download the ebook to your preferred device

ISBN 9781631959820 paperback
ISBN 9781631959837 ebook
Library of Congress Control Number:
2022939001

Cover and Interior Design by:
Chris Treccani
www.3dogcreative.net

Morgan James PUBLISHING **Builds** with... **Habitat for Humanity** Peninsula and Greater Williamsburg

Morgan James is a proud partner of Habitat for Humanity Peninsula and Greater Williamsburg. Partners in building since 2006.

Get involved today! Visit MorganJamesPublishing.com/giving-back

Dedication

For Richard Kelley (June 29, 1953-March 18, 2021)
and
Jan Vanderheiden Jimenez (July 24, 1964-September 15, 2020)

Acknowledgments

First, I'd like to thank my husband, Joel, for his courage in walking the city streets with me during the pandemic. Maggie Wright, I'm especially grateful that you let me into your life, and eventually into your heart. You are an inspiration for all homeless people. I am also beholden to all the other homeless men and women who are part of this story. They shared their stories with us and opened their hearts to our love. Next, many thanks to Maggie's mother who helped me understand Maggie. To my early readers—Joel Rosow, Ron Hall, Peter Richardson, Linda Hedgy, Anne Stembler, Gail Gessert, Carri Rubenstein, Susan Suslow, John Boselli, David Hancock and Ann Campanella—your input and suggestions were invaluable. To my editor, Sarah Saffian, as always, your skill is unmatched. My proofreader, Danielle Gasparro, who never misses a comma, thank you. To Bonny Fetterman, thank you for believing in this story when no one else did. Last, but not least, much gratitude to the MJ team.

Author's Note to Readers

This is a work of nonfiction. Most of the events took place between March 2020 and October 2021. The names of the homeless people and their case workers have been changed to protect their privacy. The characters are representative of the group of homeless people my husband and I befriended during the COVID-19 pandemic. Following each chapter is a journal entry written by one of the homeless women we met. She shares the story of her descent into homelessness and her rise out of it. Her pen name is Maggie Wright.

The test of our progress is not whether we add more to the abundance of those who have much; it is whether we provide enough for those who have too little.

--PRESIDENT FRANKLIN DELANO ROOSEVELT

CONTENTS

MAGGIE WRIGHT, JANUARY 2022

Professor Barrett entered the room and smiled at me. She had a kind face, which put me at ease. As we went around the room and introduced ourselves, I wondered what I would say when it was my turn to speak. Should I tell my fellow classmates who I really was? A homeless woman. At least I was no longer living on the street. I took a deep breath. I could do this. I was back in college, back on the road to reclaiming who I once was. Nothing could stop me now.

PROLOGUE

The first time I saw Maggie she was busy sweeping the most unlikely place—the sidewalk on the corner of Park Avenue and 30th Street. New York City's natural hum seemed to go silent as I paused to take in her appearance: tattered clothes, dirty stocking cap, shifting gaze. But it was her hands that held my attention. Covered in grime, tightly gripping the handle of a broken broom, she was intent on sweeping the area around her makeshift home, as if this one vestige of domesticity might keep her from falling into the abyss that had become her reality.

I reached into the back pocket of my jeans for a few dollars. As she accepted the offering from my outstretched hand, our eyes met. I could see her inner light flickering for an instant, defying her broken appearance before she turned and walked away.

What was it that made me stop and look at her, this one particular woman on this one particular day? I'd seen so many homeless people in the city that spring. I told myself there was not much I could do to help. Especially now. Especially in the middle of a raging pandemic. I assuaged my guilt by giving a few dollars to some of the men and women I passed by.

As one day melded into the next, I began having difficulty sleeping. Tossing all night in my comfortable bed, I knew I should share the truth about the plight of the homeless men and women who had no beds that spring—the relentless winter cold, their hunger, the ambulance sirens that disturbed their fragile sleep, and their fear, which was as contagious as the virus itself.

The divisive nature of the pandemic was evident from the beginning. Once fellow comrades in battle, as the weeks and months passed, friends, and even family members, became potential sources of the virus. The homeless, due to their living conditions, were especially feared.

Still, somehow, in the midst of the suffering, the starvation and deaths we would witness, the personal tragedies we would face, there endured a fragile and elusive, yet omnipresent, hope.

And in the center of that hope, there was love.

■ – ■ – ■

MAGGIE WRIGHT, APRIL 2020

"Good morning, Maggie." Like clockwork, I heard Pierre's voice rousing me from my sleep. "Go get yourself a cup of coffee—it's chilly out here this morning," he bellowed, as he handed me two dollars. I laughed as I gathered up my makeshift bed in front of Pierre's workplace, which was also my home, located on the corner of Park Avenue and 30th Street.

Pierre was the superintendent of the building, and thus, tasked with making sure I was gone before the workers arrived at nine o'clock. This was why I chuckled. His gesture, as always, was two-fold. While I knew he didn't begrudge me the early morning warm up, it was just a catalyst to get me up and moving. The joke was always on him—I got free coffee from the cart on the corner every morning. He didn't know this. His money was just a jump start to my day.

But I digress. This was before the pandemic hit, before one of the world's busiest cities shut down. After that, there was no Pierre, no morning coffee, no one going to work. Even though the city was deserted, I tried to respect our neighbors—what few we still had—even after Pierre stopped nudging me to get up.

I started by tidying up. I grabbed my broken broom and began sweeping the sidewalk. I had done this every day for what felt like an eternity. Three weeks on the street is a long time. Three years is a lifetime.

Since COVID arrived, barely anyone has paid attention to us homeless people, so I could have skipped my sweeping routine. But I didn't. As I made my way towards the corner, making sure I swept every bit of the sidewalk, I "felt" her presence even before my eyes could register that there was a woman staring at me, hand outstretched.

Years on the street had taught me to not trust anyone. I was desperate, so I accepted the money, warily. Why was she helping me? Why was she not afraid to come near me? Everyone else seemed to think we had the virus. I was too hungry, and desperate, to give it much consideration that morning. I thought I would never see her again anyway.

PART ONE

The best way to find yourself is to lose yourself in the service of others.

--GANDHI

CHAPTER 1

The Gathering Storm

———◼———

On March 18, 2020, we entered the nearly-deserted airport lobby. No one was even waiting in the security line. But the airport employees were there behind the check-in counters. They did not have a choice. No work meant no paycheck, which, for many locals, meant no food.

My husband, Joel, and I had been on vacation in Turks & Caicos. Just a few days earlier, the only concern I'd had was putting on enough sunscreen to ensure that my sun-damaged, freckled skin would not burn. Before the day was over, however, that reality had disappeared when rumors of an allegedly deadly virus, food shortages, and imminent border closings started circulating up and down the expansive Grace Bay beach.

We'd discussed the pros and cons of staying on the island versus returning home. Home was New York City—the nation's first epicenter of COVID-19. The island's borders were still open, but we saw the first signs of panic buying. Turks was dependent on supplies arriving by plane or ship, and both forms of travel were being cancelled on a daily basis.

Our daughter, Kyra, suggested we should consider coming home before the borders closed. Our son, Chad, was worried that if we did return, one or both of us would get COVID. We weighed the odds of getting stuck in a place with insecure food supplies versus catching the virus in New York.

The decision was binary—stay or leave.

We decided to take our chances in New York City and waited patiently to board one of the last aircraft that was allowed on the small island before its borders closed. The boarding process lasted only a few minutes.

Even though "social distancing" had not yet become a household term, it was a reality as we flew home in silence. Despite the quiet, there was a discernible negative energy on the plane—a mixture of fear, panic and irritation.

Three hours later, we landed at John F. Kennedy International Airport. By the time we disembarked, there were almost 3,000 cases of coronavirus in the city, 463 people had been hospitalized and twenty had died. Getting through Customs and Immigration took less than a minute. That airport was deserted too.

"Welcome home," the immigration inspector said, greeting us with a somber smile. "You made it."

"Is it as bad as people are saying?" I asked, afraid of his answer.

"Even worse," he replied.

We headed toward the empty taxicab line and jumped into the first one we saw. Our driver appeared confused and disheveled. Oh boy, I thought as we made our way home through the deserted highways and streets. A journey that often took over an hour was less than twenty minutes. *Here we go. It's going to be a bumpy ride.*

When we pulled up in front of our apartment on 38th Street, the building was dark and lifeless. All but two of our co-op's nine residents had left the city for surrounding areas that were perceived to be safer. I tossed my suitcase on the bed, changed into my pajamas and headed toward the living room at the front of our apartment. I looked out the window at the once thriving, now deserted Park Avenue. The city had a gray, ghost-like appearance and feel, almost as if it were the aftermath of a war. Still. Lifeless.

An eerie silence blanketed the streets and sidewalks. A lone pigeon landed on my windowsill and stared at me. The bird's eyes held an expression I did not recognize at the time but would come to know from the squirrels' faces I would see in the deserted parks in the coming weeks and months.

Hunger. The animals in New York City are dependent on people eating—and dropping—food in the parks, on the sidewalks, in the streets. They are not domesticated animals, yet they are not quite wild either.

As I fell asleep that night, I was afraid of the dark for the first time since I was a young girl. Despite my fear, however, I was aware that I was lucky. I was warm and safe, unlike the group of homeless people I'd seen bedding down for the night by the church on our street corner.

The next morning, even before I'd finished unpacking, I went out to buy some eggs and milk. Walking through the streets, I saw few cars and even fewer pedestrians. Most stores, other than the groceries and pharmacies, were closed, many were boarded up. It wasn't necessary to stop for traffic at a street corner; I could cross in any direction—even diagonally—without waiting for the *Walk* sign to appear.

What I did see, however, were homeless men and women. *Were there actually more than usual or was I just noticing them because there were so few other people?* As I passed by, I paused to look at their faces. Crooked grimaces revealed their truths—hunger, confusion, fear. By the time I returned home I felt unsettled, although I was unsure why.

I tried to focus on small tasks that afternoon, but the images of the homeless men and women distracted me—their dirty faces, empty panhandling cups, tattered clothes. With so little foot traffic in the city, their ability to beg for money was virtually eliminated. It occurred to me that while I and most of my colleagues were able to continue working remotely, so many vulnerable citizens were cut off from any possibility of making a living—restaurant workers, hair stylists, manicurists, gig workers, and also panhandlers—people who did not earn a salary, rather were paid by the job, the hour, the tip, the handout.

Even before the pandemic, before the protests, before George Floyd's graphic death, the inequality between the haves and have-nots had become a weekly topic of conversation in our house. Joel and I had numerous discussions about the country becoming a two-tier society in which the rich were getting richer and the poor even poorer. Nevertheless, I didn't know what I was going to do about any of it that afternoon.

But what I did know—what we all knew—was that the virus was real and it was in the center of our world. New York alone had more cases, more hospitalizations and more deaths than any other place on the planet. And half of the state's cases were clustered in the city—on our streets, in our buildings, in our homes.

What I also knew was that while being homeless in New York City was never an easy life, during the pandemic it had become a challenge to even eat, much less survive.

I awoke the next morning to another brutally cold day. Despite being the first day of spring, New York City was still in the grip of winter. In fairness, the city is not known for the beauty of its springs. Many years the winter turns to summer in a week's time. Nevertheless, despite having lived there for over forty years, I was not used to it, having grown up in Virginia where spring arrives by early March.

Joel and I had met the summer before I started law school in his office—in his actual office—in Washington, D.C. He was a federal mediator working at the Federal Mediation and Conciliation Service. I was a first-year law student. I'd landed a summer job tabulating labor statistics, and Joel's office had an extra desk in it. Before the summer was over, we'd become a couple. When Joel was reassigned to the New York City office, I transferred schools, and we packed up our few possessions and headed north.

Now, after forty-three years in the city, we were New Yorkers. We set out from our apartment that early spring morning with no destination or specific purpose in mind. As had become our custom when taking walks, we took a few dollars from the jar on our kitchen counter where we kept single bills for tips.

Even before the pandemic, there was an on-going debate about giving money to the homeless. Some New Yorkers were against it, believing the money was used to buy drugs and booze. The other contingent believed that a few dollars here and there was a good compromise between supporting possible bad habits and just walking by the most vulnerable city residents without an acknowledgement of their suffering.

After only three blocks, our pockets were empty. Again, I wondered whether there were actually more homeless people in our neighborhood, or if the near total desertion of the city streets made their presence more obvious. Regardless, we needed more dollars, but not a single bank was opened.

The outside ATMs were available, but the smallest bill distributed was a five. I didn't think Joel would support this expenditure, and to be honest, I was not comfortable with that amount, either. I proposed a compromise.

"Let's get twenty five-dollar bills. When they're gone, we'll call it a day."

"That's a good plan," Joel agreed.

An hour later, our pockets empty, we headed home. Joel voiced what I was thinking.

"I've never seen so many homeless people."

"I know. I noticed them yesterday when I went to the grocery store."

The next day we debated going out again. Joel was not as eager as I was. "We're supposed to be sheltering-in-place."

"I know, except Governor Cuomo specifically said we were allowed to go out for exercise. We're walking. We're exercising."

"I don't think we should be out on the streets so much. What if one of us catches the virus?"

"The chances of us catching the virus on the deserted streets is not very high. Besides, you've seen the homeless people. They're hungry. What are our options? I mean, really, what choice do we have?"

"Yeah, I agree. But every time we go out on the streets we're taking a risk."

"I know. But every time we don't go out on the streets, some of them will not eat that day. I have to live with myself when this is over. If we weren't here in the middle of it all, it might be different. We wouldn't see it. But we are here, and we do see it. I can't just watch them starve from the safety of our windows and do nothing."

Joel sighed. A deep, prolonged, mournful sigh. "How long do you propose keeping this routine up?"

"Until the streets are not so deserted and the homeless can panhandle again."

"Okay, so just to be clear, this is not our permanent new mission, right?"

"No, I don't think my feet or my wallet could survive that," I said in an effort to lighten the mood. In my heart, however, I knew we were in it for the long haul. I never felt it was our sole responsibility to take care of the homeless population during the pandemic, but I also knew they needed the support of every person who was willing to help.

Joel and I were just two ordinary people. And we were scared.

But the circumstances were extraordinary.

We continued to roam the city every morning handing out a few dollars to each homeless man or woman we passed. Most days we'd walk five to eight miles depending on the route we took and how sore our legs and feet were. In the afternoons, I'd do my legal work and Joel, a licensed mental health counselor, held video sessions with his clients.

On Friday, March 27th at 7:00 p.m., we had just settled down in our living room to watch *Jeopardy* when we heard a roar outside our windows. I jumped off the sofa and stuck my head out the window. Above the deserted street, person after person leaned out their windows, clapping and screaming *Thank you!* to New York City's health care workers. I was surprised at the number of people I saw. Up until that moment, I'd thought the city was virtually deserted.

As the nightly tributes continued, the noise increased. People banged on pots and pans, shouted through megaphones and blew through toy horns. Those two minutes of tribute became the highlight of our day, reminding us that thousands of essential workers were risking their lives to protect ours. The scene was nothing short of bone-chilling. I grabbed my phone and captured it on video to remind myself of the sacrifices being made by so many.

The following morning, we set out in a westward direction and then uptown toward Times Square, which was eerily quiet and empty. Other than the homeless, we did not see another New Yorker.

An hour later, we passed by the closed New York City Public Library on Fifth Avenue at 42nd Street. The library is an imposing white structure, reminiscent of a temple in ancient Rome, replete with enormous columns and two statues of lions seemingly guarding each side of the entrance. I wondered how many other times since it was established in 1895 it had been shut down. Even though closed, it wasn't deserted— there were numerous homeless people sitting on its steps and at little tables surrounding the exterior, most with dazed looks on their hungry faces.

We were trying to socially distance as we walked the streets, so rather than go into the enclosed area I leaned over the concrete balustrade surrounding the library and offered a few dollars to the homeless man sitting at a nearby table. He accepted the money with a confused yet grateful smile. He immediately stood up. I watched him walk across the street to a bodega, one of the few that were open that March.

As we made our way toward our apartment, we saw a homeless man urinating into an abandoned phone booth, and another, pants halfway down with his back propped up against a building wall for support, defecating. I'd seen my fair share of men urinating on the city sidewalks, but I'd never seen anything like this. I wondered if the men were freely relieving themselves because the streets were deserted or because everything was closed and there were no available public bathrooms.

"Oh boy," I said as we skittered by. "This situation is getting worse by the day." Joel, uncharacteristically silent, only nodded.

After walking two blocks farther east, we were back on Park Avenue. I spotted another man bent over inside an old phone booth. *Oh no! Not another one.* As we approached him, however, it became clear that he was not urinating. Sensing our presence, he turned around, and needle still in his left arm, collapsed to the sidewalk. As his eyes rolled back in his head, he started foaming from the mouth.

Joel ran down the street looking for a policeman. I called 911. My call was answered immediately. As I hung up, I spotted Joel running back up Park Avenue, panting and out of breath.

"I couldn't find a policeman," he shouted.

"That's okay. I got right through to 911. An ambulance is on its way."

At the time, empty ambulances were stationed every few blocks to answer emergency calls from virus victims. Two minutes later, one pulled up to where we were standing. We knew the paramedics would not want or need our further help. We pointed to the man on the ground and left. As I crossed the street, I looked back over my shoulder and saw one paramedic on his knees administering mouth-to-mouth to the victim while his partner appeared to be checking the man's vital signs.

"God help us all," I said over and over as I stumbled home. It would become my mantra for the next one hundred days.

Thankfully, I had no way of knowing that what we witnessed that morning would become our new normal or that our finely-constructed reality would soon shatter.

Maybe it was a curse. Maybe it was a blessing. It would be a long time before I had an answer. And when it came, unbidden but welcome, it would cause me to question every truth I held self-evident.

■ — ■ — ■

MAGGIE WRIGHT, MARCH 2020

I was so cold. So hungry. There was no food. No money. How were we going to survive this? If we didn't die from the virus, we'd certainly starve to death.

CHAPTER 2

March Madness

———■———

By the end of March, we both knew that we needed to concentrate our efforts to aid the homeless on a smaller area of the city. "We're spreading ourselves too thin by walking helter-skelter and not really making a difference to anyone," I said.

Joel agreed. "So, where do you want to go?"

"I've seen a lot of homeless people on Park Avenue between our apartment and 30th Street."

"Really? What do they look like?"

"Well, there's that young, red-headed man in his late twenties or early thirties who panhandles on 37th Street—the tall guy with the sign that reads *homeless and hungry.*"

"Oh, I know who you mean, but it looks like something isn't quite right with him."

"I'm guessing that most people don't end up homeless if everything is okay in their lives."

"That's true." Joel agreed. "Who else?"

"There's that couple who have created a makeshift home on the corner of Park and 30th."

"Which couple?"

"They're white. She's very short. He's about average height. Look to be in their thirties or forties. And their friend who often hangs out with them—the nice-looking Black man who is always smiling."

"Oh, right, I know who you mean."

"And just one block south in those abandoned phone booths is an older Black man sitting with a blanket on his lap, and a young Black woman is often next to him."

"Right, I know the man you are referring to. He's the one who says, 'Much appreciated' when you put a dollar in his cup." Joel said. "Do you think they actually live in those telephone booths?"

"I think so. It seems like all their stuff is in bags beside them. The other day I noticed the woman pulling a folding chair down from the top of the telephone booth. I guess that is where she stores it when she leaves."

"And sometimes there is that middle-aged, very thin, Hispanic man who walks by and talks to them for a few minutes."

"The guy who is always moving around so fast with his arms flapping?" Joel asked.

"Yes, he's the one. So why don't we concentrate our efforts on those ten blocks of Park Avenue?

"Okay, that sounds like a good plan," Joel agreed.

Park Avenue is one of the nicest streets in Manhattan and one of the few with traffic running in both directions. A combination of residential buildings and retail spaces border the wide, tree-lined boulevard, which stretches down to Union Square Market on 14th Street, twenty-four blocks south of where we live. During the first month of the pandemic, the market became a resting spot and a respite for us during our long walks. There were merchants selling farm-grown, spring vegetables, honey, cheese, apples, and farm-raised meat and fish.

There were also other New Yorkers strolling around the market, and for the most part, they did not appear to be afraid of an outdoor venue. Dr. Fauci had advised the general public *not* to wear masks claiming, "There is no reason to be walking around with a mask," and the Surgeon General, Jerome Adams, agreed, declaring, "Stop buying masks! They are not effective in preventing the general public from catching #Coronavirus." In light of this advice, we could see people's faces, and we smiled at one another as we passed by, resolute and determined, despite the obvious concern we all shared.

On Monday morning, March 30th, we headed downtown where we heard a distant roar from the New York City Harbor. The promised Navy hospital ship, the *USNS Comfort*, arrived to great fanfare and, unfortunately, to many spectators without masks who were not socially distancing. The ship had 1,000 hospital beds and 1,200 personnel onboard who were earmarked to treat non-coronavirus patients so the local hospitals could focus on COVID-19 victims. Hope had arrived, and many New Yorkers breathed a collective sigh of relief.

Later that night, we decided to do some research and educate ourselves about homelessness. Joel found a basic fact sheet produced by the Coalition for the Homeless, one of New York City's oldest agencies dedicated to serving the city's homeless population.

According to the agency's website there were 60,422 homeless people in New York, including 13,861 homeless families with 20,494 homeless children sleeping in the city's shelters, an increase of 133 percent since 2010, and the highest statistic on record since the Great Depression. In addition, thousands of other unsheltered homeless people, like the ones we were encountering, slept on the streets or on the subway cars and platforms. While life had been difficult for them before the pandemic, now their survival was all the more threatened.

The fact sheet indicated the primary cause of homelessness among families to be lack of affordable housing, with the major triggering events being eviction, domestic violence, job loss and hazardous housing conditions. In contrast, among single adults, the primary causes were noted as alcohol/drug abuse and mental illness.

The next morning it was raining, and we were tempted to skip our walk. It seemed as though we both had the same idea at the same time, however, because without exchanging words, we put on our coats, grabbed our umbrellas, and set out. When we returned later that afternoon, neither of us had one. There were others who needed them more.

As we walked into our apartment, I looked at my phone and read some good news. Mayor de Blasio had just announced that beginning on Friday, April 3rd, New York City was expanding its free meal service at schools to include all New Yorkers, regardless of whether they had children. Nevertheless, the free meals were only available Monday through Friday, leaving the hungry to scramble for food on the weekends. It was better than no meals, however.

While my morning walks and efforts to help the homeless induced an inward humanitarian focus, my legal work in the afternoon continued to connect me to the business world. I zigzagged between the two opposing realities.

A battle for where to invest my brain, if not my soul, had begun.

Battle or not, we continued walking. Keeping our distance, we skittered by them, content to be handing out a few dollars here and there. I think we might have even felt a little proud, as much for not giving into the fear of the virus as for the money we shared. We also owned the guilt we felt as we wondered couldn't society do a better job for the homeless? Couldn't we?

Then one day, I stopped to really look at Maggie, the woman who lived on Park Avenue and 30th Street as she busily swept the sidewalk. Later that afternoon, I found myself thinking about her while trying to concentrate on work. The next morning, I set out with the intention of finding her.

As we approached 30th street, Maggie was nowhere to be seen. However, we met the middle-aged man who appeared to be her partner on the same corner. Joel offered him a few dollars, which he accepted with a surprised expression and grateful smile.

"Thank you. My name is Rick."

"I'm Joel, and this is Traci."

"Can I have a dollar for Maggie, please?"

"Who is Maggie?" Joel asked.

"My wife."

"Where is she?"

"She went to look for something to eat."

Joel and I were hesitant to give Rick more money, but we thought Maggie might be the same woman I'd connected with the day before. Joel handed him another few dollars.

I saw Maggie again the next day. She was sleeping on her makeshift bed, snuggled in Rick's arms. I hesitated as I walked by, torn between the opposing desires to give her money and not to disturb her. I'd already learned that sleep did not come easily to the homeless—one eye open, one ear listening, their intermittent rest akin to sentry duty.

Sensing my presence, Maggie stirred and opened her eyes. Her hazy gaze landed directly on me and she smiled faintly when she recognized me. I quietly approached and handed her a few dollars. The money quickly disappeared up her sleeve as she closed her eyes to return to sleep.

The following day, Maggie and I spoke for the first time.

"Do you know why the money is so important to us?" she asked.

"To buy food?"

"Well, that too, except we can get food at the drop-in center near here—or at the school—even though it's not very good."

"Well, what else is the money used for then?" I asked, fearing her response might be to buy alcohol or drugs.

"To use the bathroom at McDonald's," she replied.

"You have to pay to use the bathroom?"

"Not exactly. You have to buy something to be able to use it, but even a cup of coffee or tea is enough."

During the pandemic the only public bathroom available in the area was at McDonald's on Park Avenue and 28th Street. So small amounts of money represented not just sustenance, but self-respect. Sleeping on the street, panhandling for money, wearing dirty clothes, all appeared tolerable. However, for the most part, relieving oneself on the street was avoided whenever possible.

"So, what's a drop-in center? I continued. "Is that a shelter?"

"Oh, no, we don't go to the shelters."

"Why?"

"We're safer on the streets."

"Wow, really?

"Yep, people are always stealing your things in the shelters. The first night I spent in a shelter was a disaster. I woke up the next morning and my wallet was gone."

"Can't you lock up your things?" I asked.

"Sometimes people steal from the lockers, so we just sleep with our money in our pockets."

"I'm so sorry. I've heard about shelters not being safe, but I didn't realize things could be stolen too."

"That's why so many of us end up on the streets."

"Well, what's a drop-in center, then?" I repeated.

"A place where you can sleep for a night when it's really cold. It's first-come, first-served though, and they only have chairs to sleep in, not beds. At least you can sleep with your things on your lap, so they're usually safe unless you're really drunk and end up passing out."

"I guess there is a silver lining to everything," I said, in an effort to lighten the mood.

Over the next few days we got to know Maggie and Rick a little better. Maggie told us that they were distantly related, as well as romantic partners, and had known each other since childhood. She told us that Rick had been the result of an affair between his father, a Jewish dentist, and his father's Hispanic dental assistant. He'd grown up in two very different worlds, shuttling back and forth between Brooklyn and New Jersey, not fully belonging in either place. The constant moving was upsetting, and he'd started having emotional outbursts as a young child.

Rick told us the same story about his parents. He added that he'd been homeless for ten years after losing his job as a dental assistant in the 2008 economic downturn. He'd run through two bad marriages and his maximum allowable unemployment benefits before being evicted.

"Why didn't you go live with your mother or father?" Joel asked.

"I was no longer welcome," Rick confessed.

"Why?" Joel probed further.

"I'm an alcoholic. No one wants a drunk around."

Rick began his homelessness in the Bellevue shelter. However, due to fights with other residents, he was told to leave. He then bounced from shelter to shelter, always being thrown out for fighting. Rick was eventually taken in by an elderly woman. When she jumped off the roof of the building they were living in, Rick was homeless again.

After that, another agency that serves the homeless placed him in one of their transitional supportive housing facilities. He lost that room, too, due to fights. After so much turmoil, Rick decided to take his chances on the street, and to his surprise, he liked it.

"It's cold and I'm often hungry," he said. "But I'm always free."

"So, you don't want to be sheltered?" I asked, surprised.

"I wouldn't mind a single room, but I do not ever want to live in a shelter again."

"Because of the rules?"

"Those, too, but mostly because I don't feel safe there."

Rick considered himself a "line walker," a panhandler who approaches cars stopped at a red light. Before the pandemic, he made decent money, sixty to eighty dollars a day on average. On a really good day, he could make $200. With no expenses, Rick managed to make a living for Maggie and himself until the virus arrived.

"When COVID hit, everything fell apart. For the first time since I'd learned how to make money as a line walker, there were no cars to beg from. There were always cars 24/7. This was the city that never slept. But not a creature was stirring after the virus hit, and it is very scary."

"How much money can you make now?" I asked.

"Virtually nothing."

Maggie told us she was the daughter of two Jewish professionals who had retired to Florida after long and successful careers as teachers. Born into a good family and raised in Brooklyn, Maggie said she'd been given every opportunity to succeed. She was surprised to learn that I'd grown up in Virginia under modest living conditions.

"I thought you were some kind of Connecticut trust-fund baby," she said and laughed.

"No trust funds here, but I was given a good education and that is a blessing that can make a big difference in life."

"It sure can," she agreed. "I went to college too."

I wondered why a college-educated woman would end up homeless, but I decided not to ask her more about it that morning.

Maggie admitted to making many bad choices in her life, most notably related to men. "I have an uncanny knack of finding losers."

"Just about every woman I know, including myself, has a few war stories to share when it comes to men," I admitted.

"My first boyfriend was actually the security guard at my high school," Maggie added. "He was ten years older than me and extremely handsome. He had a car, and I had a complete and total crush on him. Problem was, he returned the interest. Looking back, we were not exactly discreet. We went bowling on Friday nights. We ate at the local diner, and he would drop my friends off at the end of the night. It was completely bizarre, horribly inappropriate, and prompted a lot of lying to my mother.

She knew something was up because he would randomly show up at our house. After about six months, someone must have said something, because one morning, out of the blue, he told me he'd left his job and was moving to Pennsylvania. I'm pretty sure he was fired for inappropriate behavior, but I never asked."

"Well, that was just a high school fling," I said in an effort to maintain our connection.

"True, but it gets worse from there. My tendency to make poor choices followed me to college. That's when I met David and the real trouble began. He was actually my best friend's husband. I had a relationship with him behind her back. Needless to say, after she found out she never spoke to me again. I don't blame her."

Maggie's bad judgment with men saw a brief reprieve when she married a man from New Jersey who she said got a near-perfect score on his SATs. They had two children and were living with her husband's parents.

"We were happy for a few years even though the relationship was devoid of passion," she admitted. "Then I had an emergency root canal. I was addicted after my first prescription of Percocet."

When Maggie tried to get off the drugs, she started drinking and was frequently drunk. "I have to give my mother-in-law credit," Maggie admitted. "I was drunk and picked a fight with her. She listened to everything I had to say. And then she calmly suggested it would be better for all of us if I moved out."

Maggie told me she asked her husband to leave with her, reasoning that they could afford to rent their own place. He declined.

"Why wouldn't he go with you?" I asked, suspicious that I was not being told the whole story.

"He didn't say, but I don't blame anyone except myself. I was an addict and a drunk. And I'd lost my job because of it. I was just a drain on everyone and needed to get myself together."

"Understood," I said. "But why wouldn't your husband help you find a new place?" I asked.

"He told me to just go spend the night in a hotel and that things would calm down in the morning, and then we'd figure it out."

"And were they?"

"No, it only got worse. My drinking escalated, I ran out of money, and before I knew it, my options were few."

"Did you ask to go back?"

"No. I was too proud."

"So then what did you do?"

"My mom helped me get an apartment nearby, and things were okay for a while. A few months later, I lost the apartment."

"Why?"

"Rick was actually living with me at the time. I'd found him in New York and asked him to move to New Jersey. Bad move. One night he got drunk and destroyed the apartment. The next day the landlord kicked us out."

Maggie spent her first night as a homeless woman in a nearby shelter. After her wallet was stolen, she left the following morning. She and Rick lived under the Ferris wheel on the beach in Atlantic City for a few months. When it got cold, they headed to New York City.

"He's the only reason I'm here," she said.

"Can't you both get placed in a room together?" I asked.

"No, because we're not married."

"Oh, yeah, that makes sense," I replied. "Can you maybe get a divorce and then marry Rick?"

"That might work, but I'm afraid unless I get some form of visitation rights, I will never see my children again."

I was getting cold standing on the street corner and motioned to Joel, who was talking to Rick, that it was time to leave. We headed down Park Avenue passing by the middle-aged Black man who we routinely saw sitting in the abandoned telephone booth. He was large. I guessed he was well over two hundred and fifty pounds. His legs appeared swollen, especially his feet, which no longer fit into his shoes. Sometimes a young woman sat in the telephone booth next to him. That day he was alone.

As I dropped some money into his cup, he replied with his customary, "much appreciated."

Joel stopped to talk with him. "How you doing? Do you need anything?"

The man seemed perplexed at Joel's question and shook his head. "I'm okay, I'm okay," he repeated as he gazed off in the distance.

"Well, let us know if you need anything. I'm Joel and this is my wife, Traci."

"Thank you. I'm Bob," he replied.

As we walked back to our apartment I kept thinking about what Bob had said. How was it possible that he believed he was okay? Homeless, hungry, and clearly physically challenged, he nevertheless emanated a serenity that I rarely felt in myself.

■ – ■ – ■

MAGGIE WRIGHT, APRIL 2020

I was surprised when the woman returned two days later. I was sleeping. When I opened my eyes and saw her, there was a gentleness to her that I had not noticed before. I could tell she did not want to wake me, and I appreciated the gesture. I accepted the money gratefully. As I closed my eyes and drifted back to sleep, I found myself hoping she would return again, so that I could properly introduce myself.

I was given the opportunity to do just that when she came back the following day.

"My name is Maggie."

"I'm Traci," she replied with a smile. We didn't shake hands, though. Everyone was afraid to touch anyone because of the virus.

As the days went by, I found myself shocked at how easily I was able to bare my soul to this stranger. I told her things I'd not told anyone since I'd been on the street. *She never seemed to judge me and always made light of whatever I "confessed" to her.*

I'd become guarded of my identity since becoming homeless, afraid of people finding out just how far I'd fallen. But there I was, opening up to this stranger, not only telling her about what it was like to be homeless, but telling her what it was like to be me.

And she was listening.

But I was hiding secrets from her, and this scared me. Somehow, I just knew she would find out.

CHAPTER 3

Looking for Maggie

---◼︎---

On April 6th, thirty-six days after the first coronavirus case had been announced in New York, the number of new cases crested at 6,376, hospitalizations at 1,709, and daily deaths at 590.

Panic increased.

The Javits Center opened its doors to provide healthcare to coronavirus patients. The *USNS Comfort* reconfigured itself so as to isolate the already existing non-coronavirus patients on board and allow the ship to safely accept COVID-19 victims. Medical professionals from around the country arrived daily in New York City to help out. And KN-95 masks, following a dearth in March, were finally arriving by the thousands. Local residents were still encouraged *not* to wear them, however.

As Joel and I returned home that afternoon we noticed for the first time many people walking puppies. New Yorkers were adopting abandoned dogs in record numbers since so many city residents were sheltering in place and had free time. The puppies provided emotional support and a distraction from the harsh reality of our shared pandemic life.

One new dog owner summed it up when Joel said that his puppy was a lucky little fellow. "I see you've rescued him."

"Well, actually, I think he is rescuing me," his proud owner replied.

It was then that I realized our daily rounds were not only helping the homeless but us, as well. Getting up every morning and going out on the streets, focusing on other people's needs rather than my own, was starting to produce a profound shift in my consciousness, as well as my mood. I found myself full of energy and purpose, rather than moping through the days feeling sorry for myself and our city, waiting for the pandemic to end. It was akin to a precise mathematical formula—the more I focused on others, the better I felt.

We were almost home and feeling grateful to have ended our morning rounds on a good note when we came upon a homeless man rummaging through a garbage can. He'd found a half-eaten, dirt-covered slice of pizza, and before we could give him money to buy a fresh one, he'd gobbled it down. We stood there in silence on Park Avenue, mouths agape, hearts drained of the positive puppy vibes.

"These people are still hungry despite the free food that's available at public schools," I said. "Maybe it's because the lines are so long? Maggie said she waited two hours yesterday."

"Tomorrow we make sandwiches," Joel replied.

The next morning, we turned our small kitchen into a peanut butter and jelly sandwich assembly line. We developed a system to work simultaneously. I put the bread, peanut butter and jelly on one side of the counter and then moved to the other side, out of Joel's way, where I placed the wax paper, napkins and brown paper sandwich bags. We tripped over one another and messed up more than one sandwich—sometimes two slices ending up with just peanut butter or two with jelly. Soon enough, however, we made an efficient team.

Without bothering to clean up the kitchen, we set out with our bag of freshly-made sandwiches.

"Where do you want to walk today?" Joel asked.

"Down Park Avenue to Union Square and then back up Lexington," I suggested. "That will take us two or three hours and that's enough." What I didn't say, and maybe I didn't even realize, was that I was looking for Maggie.

The first person we saw was Rick, panhandling in the middle of the street between Madison and Park Avenues. There was still a dearth of traffic in the city, and Rick made sure he approached each car waiting for the light to turn green. We stood and watched. Very few people rolled down a window to hand him money.

"Hey, Rick," Joel shouted. "Do you want a sandwich?"

Rick looked in our direction, smiling brightly. I noticed that despite his scruffy beard and dirty clothes, Rick was handsome. He had beautiful hazel eyes, a full head of dark, wavy hair and a winning smile. Although he was only in his forties, his skin had that weathered and worn look endemic to a face that had been unsheltered for years.

"Yes!" he shouted. "I'm starving! Can you give one to Maggie, too, please?" he asked pointing to where she was sitting on the opposite corner, reading a newspaper.

"Sure," Joel said. Rick touched his heart with his closed fist and patted it several times in thanks.

We crossed the street and handed Maggie a sandwich. She put down her newspaper and started eating it immediately.

"I'm so hungry!" she said. "This bread is so soft and fresh—I'd forgotten what fresh bread feels like in my mouth. Do you buy it every morning?"

"Actually, the bread man at the grocery store gave us several loaves this morning."

"Why would he do that?"

"Because he found out why we were buying so much of it. It's nice when people help. Anyway, I see you are reading *The Times*."

"Yeah, I try to read the paper every day if I can find a free one. I like to keep up on what is happening in the world."

"Maybe you can tell me what's going on, then," I joked. "I stopped reading the newspaper or listening to the news years ago. It's just too depressing."

"I agree, but I'm an educated person and I don't want to become stupid just because I'm living on the street. I have a graduate degree in psychology."

Barely able to hide my shock, I asked, "Why in the world don't you have a job, then?"

"I used to work. In fact, I've always had jobs since I was fourteen."

"Me, too," I said. "What was your first job?"

"Dunkin Donuts. I loved that job. They gave me all the unsold donuts at the end of the day. I had my first cup of coffee that summer, and I was basically eating nothing but donuts and coffee. What was your first job?"

"I worked at the town park pool at the put-put golf course handing out putters, balls and score cards. It was hotter than the dickens in that shack in the middle of July, but I made a dollar an hour and worked twenty-five hours a week. That was good money for a teenage girl in Virginia half a century ago."

"I always liked working," Maggie repeated, gazing off in the distance.

"Well, why don't you have a job now?" I repeated.

"I used to be the director of a fancy pre-school in New Jersey," she said, ignoring my question a second time. "And before that I was a recruiter at an executive search firm on Park Avenue, not far from here."

"Well, if you want me to help you fix up your resume, send it to my email," I offered. "I heard the daycare centers are looking for people because so many employees are afraid to come to work."

"What about unemployment benefits?" Maggie asked. "The word out here on the street is that some people make more money on unemployment than if they were working."

"Yeah, I think that's true in some cases, but you need to qualify for unemployment. What about a job? I'll take a look at your resume," I offered again.

"Great!" she exclaimed. "What is your email?" I gave her my personal email and she entered it into the contacts in her phone. I had a slight sense of unease as I realized Maggie could now contact me whenever she wanted.

"I'll see you tomorrow," I promised. Maggie smiled, picked up her newspaper and began reading again. As I turned to walk away I thought, there but for the grace of God go I. What was the difference between Maggie and me? We were both educated women. Why was Maggie living on the streets while I was handing her sandwiches?

Joel and I headed down Park Avenue. Bob was sitting in his booth with the younger woman beside him. We stopped and offered them sandwiches.

"Much appreciated," Bob said. He cocked his head toward the woman.

"This is Cathy. Cathy, this is Traci and Joel."

Cathy did not speak, only nodding her head in acknowledgment. I guessed she was in her mid-thirties. She was taller than me by a few inches and a bit on the husky side, although not overweight.

I was surprised that Bob remembered our names and also that he was very polite. Joel noticed the middle-aged Hispanic man hovering against the wall, located just in front of the telephone booths.

"Who is he?" Joel asked.

Rather than answer his question, Bob called out.

"Tony, come on over here and meet these nice people."

Tony approached, head lowered, feet shuffling. Tony appeared to be in his fifties. He was wiry thin, short and appeared to sort of pulsate as he moved around. Joel stretched out his arm to give Tony the pandemic handshake—bumping elbows.

"Nice to meet you," Joel said. "I'm Joel and this is Traci."

Tony nodded but, like Cathy, said nothing. A minute later, he bolted across Park Avenue without saying goodbye.

"Where's he going in such a rush?" I asked Bob.

"To his job."

"He's got a job?" Joel asked in disbelief.

Bob nodded. "He works at a bodega on Second Avenue."

"Why can't he afford a place to live then?" I asked.

"They only pay him with food."

"He doesn't get *any* money?"

"Nope."

"Is he a legal citizen?"

"Yeah, he was born in Puerto Rico and came to New Jersey with his parents when he was a young boy," Bob replied.

"That does not seem right," I said.

Cathy was staring at me intently but did not say a word. I looked over at her several times and smiled. She lowered her head in response.

We said our goodbyes promising to return the following day and continued downtown. A few blocks farther south we met a Black couple. The man introduced himself as Ed and the woman as his wife, Tammy. She smiled and snuggled up to her husband.

"This is my husband. But sometimes he makes me mad."

"Why should you be different?" I joked. Tammy burst out laughing. Joel and Ed exchanged smirks.

My joke led to reflection. Why should Tammy and Ed feel different than any other married couple, including Joel and myself? Homeless or rich, young or old, marriage can be a challenge for anyone.

Later that afternoon, I decided to go to my small law office to work. The news that the death toll in New York had surpassed 1,000, that thousands more lay in hospitals fighting for their lives, many on respirators in ICUs, and that the total number of cases had exceeded 60,000 brought to mind the time when my law partner, Peter, had fought so hard to save his own life. It had been fifteen years, nevertheless, the memory of when he had pancreatic cancer was still fresh. At the time he'd been diagnosed, ninety-five percent of pancreatic cancer victims died within three months. Peter had beaten the odds. He was alive. It gave me hope that the homeless could also beat the odds and survive the pandemic.

Our two-person office occupied the ground floor of a brownstone in Murray Hill, a historic district in the middle of Manhattan, a few blocks south of Grand Central and east of Penn Station. Five-story brownstones line wide streets, along with imposing trees that never seem to lose all their leaves even in the midst of winter. A plethora of professional offices like ours—mostly doctors and attorneys—occupy many of the first floors, zoned for commercial use.

I'd retired ten years earlier from a large, international pharmaceutical company. The decision had not been easy. I knew it was finally time, however, when Joel made his feelings clear about how my work was affecting my health. Joel is not prone to theatrics about life in general, and certainly not about my job. In fact, he almost never commented on my professional life or the long hours I invested into its success.

Peter had retired from the same company the year before I did. We'd once enjoyed fat paychecks, stock options and expense accounts. But such benefits came with deadlines, bureaucracy and stress.

Neither of our retirements lasted long, however. Anxious to stay busy, Peter and I had started our law practice in 2011. We'd picked up our first few clients who were seeking patents on a wide variety of inventions including singing hats, high-heeled shoes and even paper clips. Then we landed our first corporate client—a large European pharmaceutical company dependent on patents to protect its products from generic competition—and we were right back in the middle of high-stakes litigation.

Nevertheless, our pre-pandemic routine offered a welcome respite from our previous schedules. We'd meet in the office in the morning, work until lunch, then put in a few more hours in the afternoon. Our view, now far from the corner offices with floor-to-ceiling windows and dazzling city vistas that we'd once enjoyed, was a bedraggled backyard garden where the birds chirping provided a welcome distraction from the noise of New York City traffic. But there was no traffic that particular morning. And a lunch outing was out of the question. The restaurants were closed.

Peter was not only alive that year, he was also sixteen years out from his diagnosis, making him one of the longest pancreatic cancer survivors in the world. As we worked in silence that afternoon, I looked up from my computer screen more than once at a man in good health who, at seventy-eight years old, was still making a valuable contribution to the legal profession. He seemed to know what I was thinking because he smiled when our eyes met. Gratitude flooded our small office, giving me goose bumps on my arms. Peter was alive, we were both virus-free, and the naval ship had finally arrived!

Nevertheless, I was emotionally and physically drained and found it difficult to concentrate on work. Peter noticed my inability to focus.

"Why don't you write a magazine story about what you are seeing on the streets? Get it down on paper and out of your head."

Maybe it was Peter's reference to getting the story out of my head because that night I was unable to sleep, distracted by thoughts of writing a story. I got up at 3 a.m. and wrote a first draft of an article about the homeless plight we were witnessing. I never submitted the piece anywhere, however, afraid it might actually be published and in turn engender the disapproval of my friends who did not yet know how we spent our mornings.

While neither Joel nor I were taking unnecessary chances, I'd started to suspect, as inconceivable as it sounded, that I'd contracted the virus when we'd been on vacation and might still have the antibodies. I shared my suspicion with Joel.

"Have you seen the list of COVID symptoms?"

"Yeah, why?"

"I had every single one of them when I was sick in Turks, even that odd one—the loss of taste and smell."

"Wow, that's right, you did. You'd eat a few bites on your plate and then give the rest to the dog."

"If I had it, I bet you had it too. Even though you weren't as sick as I was, you were definitely sick."

"I hope you're right," Joel said. "It would sure make walking around on the streets with the homeless people a lot less scary."

At the time I'd gotten sick, I had not yet even heard of the coronavirus and so just assumed I'd had a bad flu. The virus—whatever it was—had hit me in the middle of the night. I woke up with a raging fever and chills that caused my teeth to chatter uncontrollably. I almost woke Joel to ask him to take me to the emergency room, except I knew I lacked the strength to get there. Instead, I opted to get two ice packs from the freezer, one for my forehead and the other for my chest, which felt like it was on fire. I stumbled into the bathroom and popped two aspirin and an old antibiotic that I had in my suitcase from a previous trip before collapsing back into bed.

I was unable to leave the condo for two weeks, and the following week, was barely able to drag myself down to the beach in the late afternoon to sit by the ocean for a few minutes. At one point I became so desperate to get better that I listened to a local's advice and drank the ocean water. All that accomplished was several hours of vomiting.

I had a fever every day and a cough that was so persistent I had to keep a lozenge in my mouth at all times, even while I was sleeping. The loss of taste and smell made eating surprisingly difficult. I survived on Joel's homemade apple pie for three weeks, something I could not resist, even tasteless. I'd not yet taken the test for the antibodies, however, so I was not sure.

Despite my suspicion that I'd had COVID, I stopped telling people. The reaction was invariably the same—did I have proof? It was odd. It was the only time in my life that I'd been sick that I was required to provide proof of what I'd had. I decided to get an antibody test when they became widely available.

We decided to take our first trip upstate on Easter to visit our daughter, who had vacated her apartment in the city and was living at our summer house. Before we left, we made our morning rounds. That's when we met Mr. Banks, a tall, distinguished, elderly gentleman walking up Park Avenue. The city had closed the main thoroughfare for ten blocks beginning at 34th Street to provide an expansive area in which everyone could stroll, ride bicycles, walk the city's new puppy population or allow children to ride bikes or scooters. With so little traffic in the city, no one seemed to object to the partial closure of what had once been one of the main north-south boulevards in the city.

As we approached Mr. Banks, we hesitated. Despite his distinguished presentation from afar, up close, his clothes looked tattered and his hands had the tell-tale dirt stains of most of the homeless people we'd met. As we passed him, Joel slipped some money into his hand.

"Praise be to God, the Lord has risen," Mr. Banks bellowed in delight.

"He has risen, indeed!" replied Joel, despite his Jewish upbringing. It was, after all, Good Friday.

Over the next few weeks we got to know more about Mr. Banks. He claimed to be an attorney who owned a rental building in Brooklyn. He told us he'd graduated from Fordham University. Not wanting to pry, we never asked him why he wasn't living in one of his own rental units.

Our weekend visit with Kyra was all we had hoped it would be—a much-needed, albeit short, break from the depressed atmosphere in the city. Although still cold, there were signs of spring everywhere—the daffodils, tulips and cherry blossoms were sprouting forth in abundance. The numbers of new cases, hospitalizations and deaths were falling. It appeared as though the virus was on the wane.

Naively, I believed the worst was behind us.

■ – ■ – ■

MAGGIE WRIGHT, APRIL 2020

It was already 8:47 a.m. and I'd been begging for an hour. I had $1.28 in my cup. Since the city shut down, "rush hour" did not exist. There were no longer throngs of people on their way to their offices, coffees in hand, dropping change in my cup. My belly rumbled as I looked down at my empty cup and sighed. Breakfast would not come anytime soon.

I'd begun looking forward to Traci's arrival each morning. As I sat on the corner panhandling I found myself looking up Park Avenue for the familiar sight of her and Joel approaching. It had become the highlight of my day. I was surprised to find I'd quickly come to consider Traci my friend, a true rarity on the street.

I knew I could count on her for a few dollars. And the sandwiches! Even though I'd lost my sense of taste and smell years earlier due to a bad fall on the sidewalk, I eagerly awaited the peanut butter sandwich they delivered each morning. The bread was so soft and fresh, and they always used the "good" jelly, which to me meant anything other than grape. Food was scarce because the city was so empty, but you could count on those sandwiches every morning. They were a Godsend.

What was not a Godsend, however, was the fact that as Traci and I got to know each other, she began asking more questions. As I opened up to her about my past, she asked me why I could not get a job and offered to help me with my resume. This was something I thought about daily, but I was too ashamed to tell her why I could not do that. Instead, I told her I would send the resume. I never did.

How could I get a job when I slept on the sidewalk? I had no address, no bank account, and only one New York State ID card. There was no alarm clock to wake me up, not that I slept much at night anyway. Then of course there was the fact that I had no shower to get into in the morning, no clean clothes to put on, and only one single pair of ratty old shoes that were two sizes too big and falling apart. If I sent her my resume, she would have wanted me to go on interviews, and I was not ready to admit to Traci, much less to myself, just how far down I'd fallen.

If someone had told me three years ago that I'd end up homeless, I'd have told them they were crazy. I was married with two children and a good job. But about that college degree...well, that was one of the secrets I was keeping from Traci.

CHAPTER 4

New Friends

———■———

We returned to the city with noticeably less swollen feet and set out with renewed vigor, pockets full of Easter candy to share with our homeless friends. That's when we learned another lesson. Many of the homeless men and women we encountered did not have many teeth. While a soft peanut butter sandwich was a welcome treat, hard, chewy candy was out of the question.

When we arrived on their corner we found Maggie and Rick waiting for us, along with several of their friends—William, Henry, Wayne and Michael—all anxious for one of our sandwiches. We stayed on the corner for a long time that morning getting to know each person.

William was a forty-two-year-old Black man. His mother's heritage was a mixture of Native American and French. His father was Black. He told us he had a wife, children and a house in New Jersey.

He said his wife had kicked him out three years before we met him due to his constant infidelity—William had seven children between the ages of twenty-four and twenty-seven, birthed by three different women. He was a good-looking and charismatic man with a dazzling smile and an infectious sense of humor. I could see that he had a charm with women even on the streets.

Henry was sixty-two and still in good shape despite his years of homelessness. He'd once been a hairdresser with a successful business. When he was in his early twenties, Henry married a nurse, Ellen, and they enjoyed eight years of marriage. They had a nice apartment on the Upper East Side and steady jobs. At some point Henry started smoking crack and Ellen, not willing to spend her life with an addict, left him for her dentist. No one blamed her, the least of all, being Henry.

Michael was a handsome, twenty-eight-year-old veteran who had recovered from the trauma of three tours of duty in Afghanistan. During his final tour he sustained multiple bullet wounds and almost died.

Wayne told us the most heartbreaking story of all—he'd lost his wife and children in a car accident. A drunk driver had ended their lives, and effectively Wayne's, on the New Jersey Turnpike several years before we met him that morning. He was the only person we met who had secured low-income housing, a nice apartment a few blocks west of the corner where Maggie and Rick lived. So, despite hanging out with his homeless friends during the day, he himself was not homeless.

"How did you manage to get a nice apartment at such a reduced rent?" Joel asked him.

"There are a few low-income apartments in most of the nice buildings," he explained. "If you make at least $15,000 a year, you can qualify for one."

"So you have a job?" Joel asked.

"No, I got a large settlement from the truck driver's company, and it is paid to me monthly because I bought an annuity with the settlement. I knew if I got a lump sum, I'd blow it."

"Wow. That was good thinking," Joel said, praising Wayne.

To his credit, Wayne always refused to take a sandwich or any money from us. "I have enough to eat. Give it to someone else."

Maggie was unusually quiet. Normally talking excitedly whenever we showed up, she remained sullen and removed. "What's wrong?" I finally asked her.

"It's my daughter's birthday. It's been over two years since I've seen her. I'm losing hope, Tray, that I will ever see her again."

"Can't you go visit her?"

"How am I supposed to do that? I can't even afford the bus fare." Then it hit me just how far Maggie had fallen. Somehow when the homeless drop out of the shelter system, they literally fall through the cracks in the sidewalk.

Joel and I finally said our goodbyes, promised to return the following day, and headed down Park Avenue. We stopped at the next block to give out sandwiches to Bob and Cathy. Tony was not there.

"Can I have an extra sandwich for Tony?" Bob asked.

Joel handed him another brown bag. Cathy was staring at me, but, as usual, said nothing. I looked at her face, caught her eye and smiled. For the first time, she smiled back. I noticed that when she did, her entire face lit up and Cathy was quite pretty. She held my gaze for several seconds, then lowered her head, as if my presence was no longer welcome. I knew better than to push my luck further.

"Do you have any family?" Joel asked Bob.

"Yes. I have a mother. She lives in the Bronx."

"Do you have a father?"

"He was a policeman and died one night at LaGuardia airport. He wasn't even working. He'd gone to pick up my uncle, but he noticed that someone was being robbed and when he tried to stop it, he was shot."

"That's awful, I'm so sorry."

"It's okay. I have a good mother. I'm her oldest," Bob said with pride. "I have a twin brother. He's a policeman too."

After talking with Bob a few minutes more, we continued downtown towards the Union Square Market. Suddenly, we heard a man shouting behind us. We stopped and turned around to see who was causing the ruckus. A young Black man appeared by our side, screaming and crying at the same time.

"They said you have sandwiches. I'm starving."

We were unnerved but handed him a sandwich anyway. He smiled, which reassured us.

"I'm Joel and this is Traci," Joel said, putting his arm around me as much in protection as identification. "We bring sandwiches every day."

"I'm Shawn," he said and turned around and walked away. We stood there staring at him until he turned left at the corner and was out of sight.

"We're in way over our heads," I said, stating the obvious.

"Hmm," Joel replied.

The next morning Shawn was waiting for us on Maggie and Rick's corner. I gave him a sandwich. Out of the blue, he pulled down his shirt collar and showed us a large, jagged scar that ran from his ear to his throat.

"Oh, wow, what happened to you?" I asked.

"Someone knifed me in a shelter a few years ago."

"It looks like someone sewed you up with fishing line." I replied.

"It's a dangerous world," he said, shrugging his shoulders while opening the brown bag to retrieve his sandwich. "Thanks so much for these sandwiches. They're really good."

We never saw Shawn again. We continued to ask the others about him. No one seemed to have any information as to his whereabouts. Many months later, Maggie finally told me the truth surrounding his sudden disappearance. It would be one of the more bizarre stories I would hear about rivaling street gangs.

By mid-April, the cold weather still exerted its dominance in the region, even though there were a few intermittent warm and sunny days. The number of new cases, hospitalizations and deaths were all still staggeringly high, but the increase was on the decline. Nevertheless, things were tightening up rather than easing down. Despite Dr. Fauci's earlier advice on face masks, Governor Cuomo issued an order requiring everyone to wear one in any public place where social distancing was not possible. This included just about any and every place in New York City with the exception of the streets, which were still fairly deserted.

The New York Times reported the new rule on April 15th. "Imposing a stricter measure to control the spread of the coronavirus, Gov. Andrew M. Cuomo said on Wednesday that he would start requiring people in New York to wear masks or face coverings in public, whenever social distancing was not possible. The order will take effect on Friday and will apply to people who are unable to keep six feet away from others in public settings, such as on a bus or subway, on a crowed sidewalk or inside a grocery store."

The result of the order was jarring. Before its issuance, the few people we saw on the streets were our friends—fellow soldiers in battle. Now, everyone was a potential threat and people began shouting at others who were not wearing masks or not wearing them properly.

The effect on the homeless was even worse. They did not know where to get a face mask and could not afford one in any event. When we saw Bob later that day he was frantic.

"I need a mask or I'm going to get a $500 fine," he said. We added masks to our bag of sandwiches. Hundreds of them.

Added to the growing divisiveness about when and where masks should be worn, there were a fair number of New Yorkers who were anxious for the city to reopen despite the mask restriction. An uncanny article written by Dr. Murphy, an emergency room doctor at St. Barnabas in the Bronx, appeared in the *New York Post* on April 27th causing the debate to escalate. "The wave has crested at 1 p.m., April 7, the COVID-19 arrivals slowed down. It was a discrete, noticeable event. Stretchers became available by 5 p.m., and the number of arriving COVID-19 patients dropped below the number discharged, transferred or deceased. This was striking, because the community I serve is poor. Some are homeless. Most work in 'essential' low-paying jobs, where distancing isn't easy. Nevertheless, the wave passed over us, peaked and subsided. The way this transpired tells me the ebb and flow had more to do with the natural course of the outbreak than it did with the lockdown."

It was clear, however, that the city would not be reopening any time soon. It was also clear, peak or no peak, mask or no mask, that the city had hit an inflection point. Some things would get better, many would get worse. But nothing would ever be the same again.

As we continued to make our daily rounds, we learned more about the homeless men and women we'd met. Bob told us he was sixty-four and that he'd been homeless for ten years. He'd played four years of college football, had a college degree in business and had worked for years as the general manager of a convenience store around the corner from his telephone booth. When the owner had died of a heart attack in 2008, Bob lost his job and his meager savings quickly dwindled. He wasn't entitled to unemployment because he'd been paid in cash. The financial crisis was in high gear, unemployment rates had skyrocketed, and thousands of applicants were competing for the few available jobs.

His elderly mother sounded like a good woman. She'd been a seamstress in her youth and lived in a two-bedroom apartment in the Bronx that she paid for with her social security income and the odd sewing jobs she still took on.

"Why don't you go live with your mother?" I asked Bob one day.

"My nephew still lives there, and we don't get along."

"Don't you have first priority to the second bedroom being the son?" Bob had no answer, simply repeating that he did not get along with his nephew.

Bob suffered from numerous health problems, most notably, his body's predisposition to retain water. The swelling in his legs and feet was so severe it impaired his mobility. One day we found him sitting in the phone booth in a wheelchair.

"What are you doing in a wheelchair?" Joel asked.

"My shoes don't fit because my feet are so swollen," he explained lifting his pant legs to show us his feet.

The next day we bought him a new pair of shoes—size 14.5, extra wide. A few days later, we delivered them to Bob's delight and Cathy's obvious annoyance.

"What's wrong, Cathy?" I asked. It was the first time she spoke to me.

"I need a pair of shoes too."

"Fine, no problem, what size do you wear?"

"Size nine, and I want men's shoes. I don't want no girl things." It was the first time that I noticed that Cathy not only appeared somewhat masculine, but also somewhat childlike. She spoke like a young girl and emanated innocence.

"I'll order them right now," I said, pulling out my iPhone to open my Amazon account.

"Do you like these?" I asked, handing her my phone.

"Yes. I want black ones." Cathy smiled.

By the end of April, we'd formed tentative relationships with more than a dozen or so people on our daily route. In addition to Bob, Cathy, Tony, Maggie and Rick, as well as their friends William, Wayne, Henry and Michael, we'd become acquainted with Kyle who lived just off the corner of Park and 37th, Mark who panhandled on 31st, and Ed and his wife, Tammy, the woman who joked about how her husband sometimes made her mad. Somehow they all knew when we were making our rounds. For a group of people seemingly cut off from society, without cell phones or easy internet access, they maintained an effective communication system.

As our relationships grew and we heard more of their stories, we learned that they needed everything: shoes, shirts, pants, belts, jackets, blankets, underwear, socks, duffle bags and even toiletries. Joel set up a GoFundMe page and within minutes of his posting it on his social media accounts, donations started coming in. The generosity of our friends helped us to buy many of the things the homeless needed.

Apart from their needs, they, like the rest of us, also had desires. Top on that list was a cell phone. With the city's new Link NYC stations located everywhere, charging an iPhone and accessing free Wi-Fi was easy. I'd never noticed these stations before even though there was one approximately every three blocks on Park Avenue.

Some items like toiletries and used clothing were available before the pandemic. Now, so many churches and agencies that offered such essentials were closed. Joel and I were unable to say no to any of their requests. After doing some investigating, I was able to buy a bunch of the old-fashioned flip phones for twenty dollars each.

The funds in our GoFundMe accounts steadily decreased as Amazon deliveries increased. Soon enough, however, we learned to shop at the Goodwill store where we could buy almost everything on their lists for a fraction of what we paid for the same items on Amazon. And to our utter amazement, some of the items we found still had tags on them!

The day I gave Cathy her new phone, she smiled like a young girl on Christmas morning.

"Can I take your picture?" I asked.

"Yes," she said. It was one of the first of the many pictures I would take of our homeless friends.

In the following weeks, however, we learned some hard lessons when a few of the items we'd purchased were sold for a fraction of what we'd paid.

Cathy's cell phone was the first item to disappear.

"Where's your phone?" I asked.

"I don't have it no more," she admitted.

"Where is it?"

"It wouldn't charge."

"Why didn't you give it to me to have fixed?" I was heartbroken. That phone was Cathy's prized possession.

"It don't charge," she repeated.

"Where is it?" I asked again. "Was it stolen?" She wouldn't answer me. She looked down at her shoes. At least, she didn't lie.

Later that afternoon I asked Maggie if she knew where the cell phone was. I could tell by the look on her face she did not want to answer the question. Shuffling her feet and pacing around in circles, Maggie said, "She sold it for five bucks and she doesn't even have an addiction."

"Do you still have yours?" I asked her, even though we didn't buy it.

"Yep, it's right here," she said, producing it from a small bag she wore around her waist.

I was heartbroken for Cathy, but grateful that, at least, Maggie still had hers.

"These people need professional assistance," I said to Joel as we walked home later that afternoon. "We're not trained in the best ways to help them, even though you're a mental health counselor."

"You're so right," Joel replied. "We need to make contact with one of the many agencies."

"They're all still closed," I said. "How are we going to do that?"

"The case workers are working remotely," Joel replied. "Maggie told me yesterday that she's in contact with hers."

"How does a case worker whose job requires interaction with their clients on the streets work remotely?"

"I have no idea," Joel said.

"And I bet they aren't going to be allowed to return to work any time soon. I think we may be on our own out here for the time being." I realized we'd gotten ourselves into something we knew nothing about and at a time when the homeless people were perhaps the most vulnerable.

What had not yet made its way into my consciousness, however, was what was happening to us. Little by little, the lines between our reality and that of the homeless people we were serving had started to blur. We were no longer afraid of them, although we did not yet realize it. At some level, we had "dropped" into a strange world that was inhabited by people that were becoming indistinct from us.

This evolution was somewhat akin to something I'd felt when I was a little girl watching Star Trek. The first time I saw Dr. Spock's ears, I thought they were the strangest thing I'd ever seen. By the third episode, those ears just seemed normal.

While my acceptance of our new homeless friends opened my heart, it also activated my vulnerability. Somehow I knew, although I could not yet define it, that I was not coming out of this life experience unchanged. Nevertheless, at some level, I also knew that I was not turning back. Despite my lingering desire to return to my pre-pandemic life, I realized that was not going to happen any time soon, if ever.

■ – ■ – ■

MAGGIE WRIGHT, APRIL 2020

While everyday on the street was hard, there were some days that were harder than others. For me, my children's birthdays were some of the worst. It seemed like only yesterday that I was giving birth to beautiful babies, and now, here I was homeless on the sidewalks of New York City, separated from them.

It was my daughter's birthday on Monday. I woke up thinking about the last time I'd seen her. It was on my birthday in September 2017. I was already homeless at that point, living on the beach in Atlantic City. Once a week my mother-in-law would bring the kids to see me somewhere in Atlantic City. On that night we sat in a dingy pizzeria eating pizza, after which they sang happy birthday to me over a smashed cupcake, with a lone candle, emblematic of my life. As I kissed the kids goodbye, I had no way of knowing it would be a very long time before I would see them again.

Had I known that I would leave Atlantic City the following week and move to New York City, I might have found the courage to beg for forgiveness. But I didn't. I was too broken.

My daughter's birthday was especially difficult in 2020. Because of the pandemic, I knew that I would have been home with my kids every day, helping with school, having extra time to just be together. I couldn't help but think about how much of their lives I was missing.

I was in a bad mood that day and didn't want to see or talk to anyone. Not even Traci and Joel, who always brightened my day. It had been over two years since I'd seen my children, and I realized that I didn't know them anymore. While I'd been sleeping on the sidewalk, begging for money and food and struggling to survive, they'd been growing up apart from me.

I waited all day to work up the nerve and finally called my husband from the LinkNYC phone across the street. He put our daughter on the phone, and I was able to wish her a happy birthday. I asked her what presents she'd gotten, and she said all she wanted was for me to come and visit her.

We only spoke for a moment, and I hung up feeling defeated and sad. I had disappointed my child on yet another birthday, simply by not being present. Not that I was in any condition to visit. I was broken, and she deserved better.

CHAPTER 5

Spirit Animals

———■———

The gyms were closed, and I was still unable to swim, something I'd been doing most of my life. Our daily rounds helped me stay active, but a long walk did not produce the same effect as an all-out, half-mile swim. I started to feel frustrated as my feet swelled, not to mention that I was used to burning off far more than calories in the swimming pool— frustration and unrest were just two of the feelings that lessened as I'd plowed my way through the water.

One day as I approached Maggie's street corner, she noticed I was limping.

"What happened to you?" she asked, clearly concerned.

"Nothing. My feet are just swollen from so much walking."

"You seem pretty athletic to me," Maggie said, confused.

"True, but I'm a swimmer, not a runner. And it's still darn cold out here so walking so much is not that pleasant."

"It's crazy. This is the only time I remember being cold in April," Maggie agreed. "Somehow the weather matches everyone's mood this spring."

"You're right, and I don't think this virus is going anywhere anytime soon."

"I agree. Anyway, you swam a lot as a kid?" Maggie asked, bringing our conversation back to swimming.

"Yep. I always loved the water, and I started swimming before I was out of diapers," I said and laughed.

"Wow, same for me! I grew up only a few miles from the beach, and my parents used to take us there a lot. Were you a good swimmer?" Maggie asked.

"Pretty good."

"Tell me about it, please," Maggie asked.

■ – ■ – ■

June 1961. I was only six when the swim coach noticed that I had a natural stroke and talked my parents into letting me join the team, even though the next youngest swimmer was eight years old. I won my first two blue ribbons at the opening meet. As I pulled my body out of the water after the second race, the coach came over and picked me up over his head. My dad smiled and my teammates cheered. Even my mother, who rarely allowed her emotions to be seen, had a smirk on her face. I think it was right then and there that the misguided thought that would control most of my life entered my consciousness—winners get attention; winners are loved.

Two years later, I made my first all-star meet. The referee summoned the race—girls, eight-and-under, swimming two lengths of the pool, backstroke. I jumped into the water, grabbed the wall and pulled my knees up into a crouched position, prepared to lunge backwards when the gun fired.

I'd trained for months for this race by working out in a wet sweatshirt to build up my strength and endurance. This threw off my timing. When I was almost to the end of the pool, I saw the flags over my lane and knew exactly where I was. Five strokes to the wall. I began to count.

One. Two. Three. Four.

Boom!

I'd reached the end of the pool one stroke sooner than I'd been doing in practice and hit my head with such force that I momentarily passed out. Despite the throbbing in my skull, a combination of anger and adrenaline helped me recover. Nevertheless, my initial lead was blown. I gave it everything I had, but when my hand hit the finish line, I was in fifth place.

Despite my disappointment that day, I kept practicing. When I wasn't working at my summer job, I was in the pool swimming—two hours each morning and afternoon. In the winters, I also practiced twice a day—two hours before school and two hours in the evening. It was a grueling schedule, even by today's athletic standards, made even more difficult by the fact that we did not have goggles to protect our eyes from the chlorine burn.

I learned some valuable lessons in the water, none more important than the day I false-started in a relay event. I'd become accustomed to the pre-race jitters and had developed a split-second precision ability to take off the moment the start gun fired or, in a relay event, when my teammate's arm lifted out of the water for her final stroke. Even though my feet were not allowed to leave the starting block until her hand touched the wall, I knew by the time it took my brain to send the signal to my body to dive, her hand would be there.

But that day I knew I'd left the starting block too soon the instant I took off. I hesitated in the water for a moment as I weighed the odds—the odds that maybe the referee had not noticed my false start against the odds that if I turned around, swam back, and retouched the wall, my team would lose anyway. My mind urged me to keep swimming. My gut was nagging me. I followed my instinct, swam back and retouched the wall, and as it would turn out, the referee had seen that I'd left the starting block too soon.

My water lessons followed me to New York City, to law school, to a large pharmaceutical company and, eventually, to the streets of the city during the pandemic. And to this homeless woman—Maggie—who stood staring at me that cold April morning, listening intently to my story. I couldn't help but wonder what experiences she'd had growing up, what lessons she'd learned, or didn't. And what made the difference in our lives? Why was she living on the streets while I slept in an apartment a few blocks away?

To my shock, despite the differences in our living conditions, I soon found myself seeking out Maggie, and other homeless people, as well, who had only months before been objects to avoid. Determination propelled me forward in an effort to help them, to a place where compassion trumped logic and courage dissipated fear, even when the outcome was uncertain. It was not at all unlike that swim race.

The money and clothes were important to our new friends, but a homemade sandwich meant someone cared enough about them to make it. We showed up, rain or shine, day after day. If we were going to visit our daughter, we told them in advance and brought extra food the day before. Tenuous connections morphed into solid bonds. Everyone began to share more details of their stories.

We learned that the young red-headed man who lived only a block away from us was named Kyle. He had just turned thirty and told us that he'd been homeless for ten years. He was originally from Arkansas. He'd become an expert at riding freight cars and had traversed the United States spending time on both coasts and everywhere in between before ending up on the streets of New York City.

One day, after a certain level of trust was established, he told us he was adopted. The next time we saw him he told us that he was fairly certain that his adoptive parents had murdered his biological ones. He was only two years old at the time.

"You mean the people who killed your parents abducted you and then adopted you?" I asked with alarm.

"Yes, my last name is different on my birth certificate."

"Why would two people who murdered your parents adopt you?"

"I don't know; I think they were afraid I could identify them to the police."

"Do you remember seeing them the day they killed your parents?"

"No, but I remember the sound of my adoptive father's truck."

"His truck?"

"Yes, even years later when he left the house, I recognized that sound. It was the same sound I'd heard the day he showed up at my parents' house."

Kyle didn't know exactly why his adoptive parents murdered his biological ones. He thought it might have been over a drug deal. He did remember the last words his biological father spoke.

"Hide him in the kitchen," he shouted to his wife as the intruders busted down their front door.

It wasn't long afterward that his adoptive parents started abusing him, and by the time Kyle was fifteen, the violence had become so extreme he feared for his life.

"I ran away because one night they both threatened to kill me."

"That's a good reason," Joel said.

"Yeah, I thought being homeless was less dangerous."

Cathy, the Black woman who lived in the abandoned telephone booth next to Bob, told us she was thirty-seven. She had a mental health counselor at Bellevue Hospital and faithfully kept her weekly appointments. From what we witnessed, she received very good care there. Bellevue Hospital is a public hospital, which prides itself on having never turned away any patient since its opening as an almshouse in the eighteenth century.

Cathy's biological father died from alcoholism when she was eleven. A few years later, her mother remarried. She was sexually molested by her father for the first time when she was six years old and physically and sexually abused by her stepfather. She was certain her stepfather had poisoned her mother when she was fifteen.

"I want to find him and kill him," she said on more than one occasion. "I had a good mama."

They'd been living in Florida when her mother died. Cathy returned to New Jersey where she was born to live with her aunt and uncle. Soon after her eighteenth birthday, having a strong preference for Florida's warmth over Northeastern winters, she returned to The Sunshine State. She became a mother at nineteen and was abandoned by her son's father. Unable to take care of herself, much less her son, her options were few.

"Is your son with his father?" I asked her one day.

"No, some family friends took him when he was three years old. I haven't seen him since."

I didn't have the stomach to ask if they had been good to him. The next day, however, I suggested she join Facebook and borrow Maggie's iPhone to search for her son.

"I can't," she replied matter-of-factly. "The Illuminati are after me."

I was speechless. I'd heard the term Illuminati in conjunction with conspiracy theories that were bantered about, but I never suspected Cathy would believe in such a group, or more importantly, that she would think they, whoever "they" were, made her a target.

Tony, the Hispanic man whose arms and legs were always in perpetual motion, had been homeless for over two decades. He worked three, two-hour shifts a day at a bodega on Second Avenue. As far as we could tell, he never missed one. He told us he slept by the police station near the Port Authority where he rented a storage unit for $70/month. He was proud to let us know that the police liked him and kept an eye on him while he slept.

Of all the homeless people we knew, Tony was the most concerned about his cleanliness. He had an uncanny knack for finding the free showers that popped up here and there around the city during the shutdown. Tony actually possessed a wealth of information about the available services for the homeless.

For the first few months of the pandemic, he was showering at a church on 30th Street on the West Side. He told us they gave him clean socks and underwear with each shower. Eventually, that facility closed down and the Red Cross opened up portable showers nearby.

Tony was also the first person to ask us to sign his "Verification of Homelessness" form. This was the first step to getting a case worker. We were surprised to learn that this was not easy. Even Tony's employer refused to sign it for him. Joel agreed to sign it on the spot. He took the form home and made fifty blank copies and then walked back downtown and delivered a signed one to Tony.

"Why do we need so many?" I asked Joel.

"I'm getting every single one of them off the street," Joel replied with conviction.

"Good luck on that mission. Some of them have been homeless for decades."

"All the more reason to help them. If not us, then who?"

Mark was a forty year old, white man who panhandled on 31ˢᵗ Street between Park and Lexington. He told us that he'd grown up in an affluent family in Connecticut but had started using drugs as a teenager. Nevertheless, he'd had a successful business and a wife and stepdaughter he adored.

One day, however, his wife suddenly died of a heart attack at age thirty-six and his world fell apart. Mark's drug use escalated, and he started stealing to support it. Within a few months of his wife's death, he was sentenced to four years in prison. His stepdaughter went to live with her grandmother.

When he was released in 2019, Mark had no family member willing to help him, a teenage stepdaughter who would no longer speak to him, a failed business, and no home. For reasons that were never clear to him, he became an outcast, even among the homeless people.

"No one likes me," he'd complain on numerous occasions. "I'm not the only addict out here."

When I asked Maggie about it she just shrugged. "He's a crack head."

"Well, it's not like Mark is the only one out here using drugs," I said in an effort to defend him.

"Yeah, I don't know. I can't stand him, though."

Several weeks after we'd first met, we ran into Mark again on our way home from making our morning rounds. He was incoherent from too much crack, but he managed to ask Joel for money. Joel refused his request.

"Mark, I can't give you money. You know that. It will go right up in smoke."

"I'm going to stop using drugs, get a job and get myself an apartment," he said with conviction

Right, we thought.

The next morning, as luck would have it (given that we were trying to connect with a professional agency), Kyle gave us the business card of his case worker, Karen, who worked at one of many organizations in the city we'd discovered that spring dedicated to helping the homeless. Karen's agency's primary mission was to provide affordable housing to homeless citizens, starting with placements in safe haven rooms. From there, if all went well, an individual became eligible for permanent, low-cost housing.

While I was busy that afternoon in my office dealing with the latest generic company challenging our European pharmaceutical client's patents, Joel was speaking with Karen on the phone and getting educated on the numerous other homeless organizations in the city. He took copious notes, and when I returned from work, he shared what he had learned.

Mainchance, one of New York's City's largest drop-in centers, assists individuals of many ages, backgrounds and cultures. Located in Murray Hill, a short walk from Grand Central Station and our apartment, Mainchance offers its clients emergency overnight shelter, medical services, and three meals a day.

The organization's name derives from "having an eye for the main chance," describing someone who is trying to improve his or her situation. Its mission is to provide people with the resources that will offer them the best possible opportunity for improvement.

"That sounds like an amazing place," I said. "But both Maggie and Rick said they won't eat the food there."

"Yeah, who knows," Joel said. "Maybe they've had bad luck. This morning Cathy told me the sandwiches are very good."

"Let's drop by there tomorrow and donate some of the free bread we're getting. We can't use it all before it goes stale," I suggested.

"That's a great idea."

When we dropped off six loaves of bread the following morning, we were met with a certain amount of suspicion. Fair enough. I'm sure the workers could not figure out why two elderly, white people had walked in the door in the middle of a pandemic.

The Bowery Residents' Committee (BRC), located at 131 West 25th Street, is one of the city's leading nonprofit organizations providing services and housing to the homeless. The BRC offers transitional and permanent housing, substance abuse treatment, mental and physical health services, and workforce development. Its stated mission is "Helping people reclaim lives lost: We restore hope and dignity by offering opportunities for health and self-sufficiency."

The Bowery Mission is a religious organization located at 227 Bowery. It offers a variety of services including social services, meals, clothing and emergency shelter. They pride themselves on building trust with those they serve.

The Coalition for the Homeless is the nation's oldest advocacy and service organization for the unsheltered population. Located at 129 Fulton Street, it provides housing, food, crisis services and job training. Believing that food, housing and a chance to work are basic human rights in a civilized society, the organization has worked for the last forty years through litigation, public education, and direct services to uphold these rights for the homeless population.

Breaking Ground is a nonprofit organization dedicated to providing high-quality transitional and permanent housing to the homeless. Founded by Rosanne Haggerty in 1990, it has two main locations in the city—one on East 28th Street and the other at 505 Eighth Avenue.

Maggie and I created a flyer listing all these services and a few others. Included on our list was St. Mary's Church on the West Side, which offered free clothing and toiletries on Wednesday afternoons, the Antonio Olivieri Drop-in Center on West 30th, and St. Bart's on Park Avenue, which provided dinner seven days a week.

Joel and I added these flyers to the items we handed out each morning and were surprised to see that many weeks later, Bob and Cathy still had their copies neatly folded and tucked away in the duffle bags we'd bought them.

One of the many things Joel and I learned handing out the flyers was that some of the homeless people, like Rick, actually preferred to sleep outside, weather permitting. Many were afraid of the shelters and even the drop-in centers, so on the coldest nights, they would descend into the subways. Even the tunnels and platforms provided enough protection from inclement weather on most nights.

We were also surprised to learn that they didn't need money to get into the subways. Young or old, healthy or frail, all were expert turnstile jumpers. How this was possible, I could not imagine, knowing of some, like Bob, who lacked decent mobility. His lack of agility notwithstanding, he was the first person to tell us about his jumping skills.

"How can you jump the turnstile?" Joel asked. "You told us you can barely walk to McDonald's to use the bathroom."

With a twinkle in his eye and a smirk on his face, he said, "I remember how to do it from my football days."

Despite all of the available offerings, taking that first step towards shifting into temporary housing was challenging. Priority for placement in one of the safe haven rooms was reserved for the most vulnerable—people with children, the old and infirm, and women in danger of physical harm. Maggie was the first homeless person we knew who ended up being placed in a safe haven room. And the reason was not a good one.

Bob first alerted us to what was happening. As we handed him a new pair of jeans, he dropped his voice to a whisper.

"She needs to go home."

"Who needs to go home?" Joel asked.

"Maggie. Rick is beating her again. This morning she was running down Park Avenue before even the birds were awake, screaming for help."

I walked to the corner where Maggie and Rick lived. I was thinking about how I was going to bring up the subject when she took my hand and whispered, "Can we talk?"

"What's up?"

Maggie hesitated, then made the rather vague claim, "Rick's a great guy, even though sometimes he gets a little handsy."

"You mean, he hits you?"

"Not exactly. He pushes me around," she admitted.

"No one can abuse you unless you allow it."

"Rick is family and I feel obligated to protect him."

"Protecting him is fine; allowing him to abuse you is something else. How long has this been going on?"

Maggie lowered her head and a tear rolled down her left cheek. "On the third day of my homelessness, Rick stopped being nice to me. He explained to me that I couldn't sit and watch him work all day. I had to make money too. He made me a cardboard sign and sat me on the corner of 30th Street and Park Avenue, right outside the bodega and told me not to get up until I made at least twenty dollars. I didn't make one cent. I was so embarrassed. I kept my head down the entire time and refused to look or speak to anyone. That was the first time Rick hit me."

"When was that?" I asked.

"Three years ago. But the next morning, I made my own sign and sat down. I must have looked so ashamed because a man stopped and gave me two dollars and a cigarette. He introduced himself and told me he worked around the corner. He promised to come back and check on me later, and I burst into tears. I couldn't believe someone was kind enough to help me.

That gave me a boost in confidence, and I picked up my head. I found a *New York Times* in a nearby trashcan and started to do the crossword puzzle to take my mind off things. A man stopped and asked me if I'd gotten eighteen across. When I told him the answer, he handed me ten dollars. Then Rick came back to check on me, and I was sure I wasn't going to get slapped again. But I was wrong."

"So to cut to the bottom line, Rick's been hitting you for three years?" I asked. Maggie lowered her head and cried for a second time, but it was not just a single tear rolling down her cheek. It was an all-out sobbing that seemed to arise from her heart, rather than her eyes. I stood there dumbstruck, motionless, like a deer in the proverbial headlights.

The next morning Maggie was waiting for me, sitting on a folding chair, reading the newspaper. Rick was panhandling in the middle of the street. We stopped to give him a sandwich.

"I'm having to teach Maggie a few things about the reality of being homeless," he blurted out.

I thought this was odd since Maggie had been homeless for three years, and by all accounts, seemed to have adjusted to it as well as anyone can adjust to living on the streets. Joel kept talking with Rick, and I headed toward Maggie, who put her paper down and jumped up.

"We need to talk," she said. "Rick beat me up *real* bad this morning."

"Was this the first time?" I asked, afraid of the answer, knowing that he'd been slapping her for the last three years.

"No, a few years ago he hit me over the head with a bat. I fell backward and ended up in the hospital for a week. The external damage healed, but I lost my sense of taste and smell, and I haven't been able to taste or smell anything since."

I was so shocked I asked a stupid question. "You can't taste the peanut butter sandwiches?"

"No, but I still love them because the bread is so fresh."

My stomach cramped as I looked over at Rick. He seemed so gentle and vulnerable talking to Joel, yet that day I was learning more about his dark side.

"Why don't you go home to your husband and children or maybe to Florida to your parents?"

Rather than answer my question, she changed the subject.

"What happened with your husband? Did he hit you, too?"

"No, no, never."

"So what do you want to do about Rick?" I said, trying to bring the conversation back to the crucial issue. Before she could answer, I had an idea. "Listen, Rick wants to sleep with you. Can you tell him no more sex if he hits you again?"

And with that suggestion, which seemed an obvious first step to me, Maggie started jumping up and down screaming, "I just met my spirit animal. She's my spirit animal!"

She was shouting so loudly that Rick and Joel stopped talking and stared in our direction. Joel looked confused; Rick looked angry. The few other pedestrians on the street stared in disbelief at Maggie bouncing straight up in the air as if she were on a trampoline.

I stared, too, but not in disbelief. I somehow knew she was going to break free. I didn't know if it was my intuition or the intensity of Maggie's reaction. Nevertheless, I was certain about this outcome.

Maggie was homeless, broke and afraid. But that day was a new beginning for her.

■ – ■ – ■

MAGGIE WRIGHT, APRIL 2020

I was surprised to learn that Traci was a swimmer. I, too, was swimming before I was walking. I was continually amazed to see how much we had in common. This did not make sense to me. How could we be similar? I was a homeless woman living on the sidewalk. Traci was some kind of a lawyer. As odd as it might sound, I felt that we were becoming friends, despite all of our differences, including our ages.

It wasn't long before Traci learned that Rick was beating me. I was filled with shame when she confronted me about it, yet I was shocked at how open and honest I was about the severity of what I was going through. I even told her about the worst beating of them all, the one that had robbed me of my taste of sense and smell, all those years ago.

By the end of that conversation something was different. That was the first time I had ever said the words out loud, "I am in a physically abusive relationship." Traci listened carefully, but then she said that no one can abuse you unless you allow it. I wondered if she was speaking theoretically, or if she had been abused, too, and by whom?

Then Traci sort of jokingly said that I should not sleep with Rick if he hit me. For some reason, this advice filled me with courage. I felt that I had just met my "spirit animal," inspiring something deep inside me. Suddenly, I started jumping up and down on the street corner.

That day was the first day of the rest of my life.

CHAPTER 6

Breaking Free

■

The change of mind and heart we experienced in helping people in need was so subtle at first I barely noticed it. When Joel and I had started walking the streets in March, our judgments and fears of the homeless were clear. Even after we had begun making our daily rounds handing out sandwiches, we still quietly perceived them as "the others." By the end of April, however, they'd somehow become our friends.

"I don't know how this happened," Joel joked on more than one occasion. "But some of our best friends are now homeless people."

"I know what you mean. And it's all the more clear because none of our other friends will see us due to the threat of COVID."

As the homeless transitioned from *others* to friends, we grew more at ease when it came to physical contact. Dangling sandwiches and dollar bills on the end of our outstretched arms were replaced by hands brushing against hands as we dispensed our daily offerings. Quite apart from the risk of COVID, some of our new friends emitted an unpleasant smell as we drew near, and we learned some had reported past incidents of head lice. However, our hearts melted as our minds opened, and it wasn't long before we sought out our new friends during our daily rounds rather than just waiting until we bumped into them.

The city was still quiet, but we saw some businesses reopening, most notably the banks which began to offer limited teller service. While the fear of the virus endured, there were signs that its peak was behind us, as reported by Dr. Murphy, the ER physician from the Bronx. Since April 7th, the day Dr. Murphy said it had crested, the number of new cases, hospitalizations and deaths in the city had steadily declined, making it apparent that the auxiliary hospitals, welcomed by large crowds in March, were no longer needed.

On April 30th, exactly one month after its arrival and docking along the Hudson River, the USNS Comfort left New York City having treated fewer than two hundred patients. There was no fanfare for its departure—it silently pulled out of the harbor and headed back to Norfolk, Virginia. The field hospital that had been set up in the Javits Center in March was dismantled the following day having treated just 1,000 virus patients. The sixty-eight tent field hospital in Central Park closed the following week.

Another polarizing debate ensued among city dwellers. One side saw the auxiliary hospitals as too little, too late, while the other praised Governor Cuomo for his preparedness. It was beginning to seem that no matter what anyone did in response to the virus, disagreement ensued. Social media posts evidenced that very few people accepted the peak had passed and the city's case numbers were actually diminishing. And those who did not dispute the numbers claimed they didn't matter—a person could contract the virus more than once and, in any event, a second wave was coming. Both predictions would prove true.

Fear increased, and with it, the level of physical protection. First, the mask options expanded. There were simple, home-made face coverings, blue hospital masks, KN-95s and even those masks with air vents on either side, used by people who handle toxic waste. Some people wore plastic shields that covered the entire face. A few even wore those and masks. Gloves also grew in popularity. We saw everything from the thin, clear plastic ones to the industrial type. We even saw people with cotton balls in their ears, presumably in an effort to avoid airborne virus particles entering the body that way.

The mask debate, in particular, continued to divide the country and New York City. While most New Yorkers wore masks, many people commented on *how* they were worn. In particular, if anyone's mask slipped slightly below the nose, someone would quickly shout out a correction. New Yorkers, once united in battle against a common viral enemy, were now potential enemies to be feared.

Later that week, another closure was announced. On May 7th, at exactly midnight, police began asking passengers to leave the subways. By 2:12 a.m. every train was out of service. The planned overnight shutdown was a watershed moment—the first time since it had opened 115 years earlier. The transit system was already reeling from record low ridership. The few times Joel and I rode the subway or the bus that spring, we were the only two people onboard. The last thing the fragile system needed was an enforced daily closure and further loss of revenue.

My first concern was for the healthcare employees who worked night shifts. How would they get home? There was a dearth of taxis and Ubers due to a lack of riders. My second thought was where would the homeless sleep? While the days were noticeably warmer, the night temperatures were still dropping below freezing despite May's arrival.

Joel and I went through the list of our homeless friends. Cathy had been going to the nearby drop-in center on cold nights, so she would be fine. Tony could sleep in his storage unit if need be, and Kyle was young and had a sleeping bag. William had recently been assigned a safe haven room. Ed and Tammy bedded down together under their blankets, benefitting from each other's body temperatures, as did Maggie and Rick. However, Henry, at age sixty-two, was a concern. Due to his age and poor health, we were especially worried about Bob. He routinely slept in the subway on cold nights. We couldn't do anything about the planned subway closure, but we did have a few spare blankets. We took them to our friends before falling into bed after midnight.

We woke up early and had the sandwiches made before 8 a.m., adding granola bars to our bag in case we ran out of sandwiches and set off looking first for Kyle.

He was walking up and down 37th Street with his hand-made, brown paper sign reading *homeless and hungry*. At six feet, five inches tall, he was hard to miss. On some days, I'd notice his long, red beard illuminated by the morning sun before my brain registered that it was him. His hair was also red, although it was usually greasy, which weakened its tendency to reflect the sunlight.

We'd already gone through our son's clothes looking for hand-me-downs for Kyle, but he was four inches taller and fifty pounds lighter than Chad. So we ended up ordering new things for him on Amazon. With donations from Joel's GoFundMe page we'd bought him a light-weight green jacket, which had arrived that morning.

When we presented the gift, Kyle immediately took off his old, dirty winter coat, donned his new spring jacket and walked over to the window on the nearest apartment building to look at his reflection in the glass. A slight smile crossed his face, for a moment diminishing his stoic countenance and the pain in his eyes.

Despite his happiness over his new jacket, Kyle was in a bad mood so Joel attempted to cajole him with a joke.

"You look really good in your new jacket, Kyle. Don't blame me if you get yourself a girlfriend." Joel's comment elicited another brief smile that quickly turned to a frown as Kyle looked off into the distance, his beautiful green eyes sparkling in the sunlight.

"I'm getting tired of this virus," he said.

"Everyone is," I replied

The homeless were especially affected by the prolonged shutdown, due to the lack of pedestrian traffic and ability to panhandle. The streets were still mostly empty and those few people who were out on them did not appear to be feeling especially generous that May.

While all of our new friends had been able to collect decent money before COVID, post-pandemic onset, they were lucky to get a few dollars a day. I did, however, notice some people offering food—sandwiches, cookies, and bottles of milk, juice and water.

The case workers were still working remotely. Joel and I were able to act as temporary go-betweens, but we were only watching out for a few dozen or so homeless people, leaving hundreds of others to roam the deserted streets.

We did our best to help the group of people we'd "adopted." We spent an hour with Kyle that morning before continuing down Park Avenue. We urged him to hang in there claiming that things would get better soon. I don't think he believed us. I don't think we believed us either. We were all starting to see the potential long-term consequences of the virus.

A once-bustling city was still eerily quiet. Most of the stores were closed and many of the businesses that were allowed to remain open, nevertheless, shut down. Finding a single bank that offered any service other than a lobby ATM remained challenging. Many bodegas were closed and new *For Rent* signs were posted daily. There was only one Starbucks for blocks around and it only offered curbside pickup.

Almost all of the dry cleaners in our neighborhood were also closed. I finally found one, but the one time I dropped something off, no one was in the store. After calling out "hello" several times, the owner who I'd never met emerged from a side staircase I'd never noticed. *Was he living in the basement of his store?* He looked disheveled and disoriented.

"Are you open?" I asked.

"Well, yes, but I'm the only one working. We have no business, so I had to let all my employees go."

"I'm so sorry to hear this. Is it okay if I give you this?" I asked, holding out my sweater.

"Yes, yes," he said as he took it and walked away.

"Wait, can I have a receipt, please?" He shuffled back over to the register on the counter, asked for my name, and handed me a receipt.

When I returned the following week to pick up the sweater, it had been lost. I never got a reasonable explanation for how it had disappeared as the dry cleaning was allegedly done on premises. Still, despite the fact that it was my favorite sweater, somehow its disappearance didn't matter. There were so many people living on the streets with no sweaters at all. I chalked it up to another casualty of the virus.

The absence of dry cleaners was not just a result of the lack of people living in the city at the time. It was also because residents were working remotely from their apartments and not wearing business attire in need of dry cleaning. The trickle-down financial impact of the shutdown was spreading outward like an inkblot. A year later, every dry cleaner in our neighborhood would be out of business.

Many companies had already informed employees that they would not be reopening until the fall. Our daughter was told that she should plan to work from home for the foreseeable future. Her husband's tech company announced it would remain closed until January. Our niece, who worked for a financial institution, was informed that her office would be closed until September. Even when she did return, there were so many positive virus tests that she was immediately sent back home to work remotely. My friend's law firm informed her that she would be working from home until a vaccine became widely available.

Still, they were among the lucky people—they had jobs and paychecks. Our nephew, a real estate agent, was surviving on unemployment. He told us what we'd already witnessed on our daily walks—people were moving out of the city, not in, fleeing for more spacious and remote locations. I'd witnessed this trend after 9/11, yet not to the extent it was happening now. After 9/11, real estate values plummeted but then recovered. Likewise, after the financial crisis of 2008 it was almost impossible to sell an apartment. Most people stayed put, however, and rode out the downturn. New Yorkers viewed 9/11 as an isolated event and the financial crisis as recoverable.

Not so with the virus. There was always another case, another hospitalization, another death. The ambulances continued to invade the stillness with their high-pitched sirens. Refrigerated vans waited eerily outside of the hospitals prepared to store bodies until funeral arrangements could be made. The fear, omnipresent and paralyzing, was more contagious than the virus.

Even doctors and dentists were hard hit. I did not see one open doctor's or dentist's office that spring despite walking hundreds of miles through the streets. When our son's friend had a dental emergency, he had to drive her to White Plains, an hour north of the city, for treatment.

The restaurant business was also decimated. Even though they were allowed to remain open for takeout, very few did. Before the pandemic, the restaurant takeout operation was thriving. The pandemic destroyed even that part of the business. People had time on their hands and less money in their pockets, so they turned to cooking. I doubted whether our friends' restaurant in Mahopac would survive. It was operating on the slightest margin five years before, when we'd still been partial owners.

The full economic fallout from the shutdown was becoming clear. The New York City we loved was dying. It was not just the COVID victims we were losing. It was our businesses, the value of our real estate, and even our way of life.

Nevertheless, most people, still unaware of the city's impending financial challenges and the long-term damage it would produce, agreed on at least one thing that May—the sacrifices we were all making were worth it to save lives. New Yorkers buckled up and doubled down, fellow soldiers in battle.

Morning after morning we'd get up early, make sandwiches and head out. Most days we'd see Kyle first because he panhandled just a block from our apartment. His proximity to us, as well as the regular interaction it allowed, continued to induce trust. Slowly, he shared more of his history.

After fleeing from his adoptive parents when he was fifteen, he was placed in a home for, as he described it, "unwanted, psychologically troubled children." That place, despite his description of it, turned out to benefit him in some ways. While living there, he earned his high school GED and completed an on-line, two-year associate degree in business.

At age seventeen, Kyle was adopted for a second time by a woman in Texas. At first he thought his life had turned around. That security did not last long. One night he awoke to find her in his bed, fondling him. Kyle left the next day, beginning an odyssey of hopping freight trains, crisscrossing the country.

He eventually settled in Louisiana where an unexpected brawl in the lobby of a Baton Rouge hotel left him passed out on the floor—one man injured, another one dead and Kyle accused of murder. Despite the hotel's video camera clearly showing that it was the injured man who had delivered the fatal blow, Kyle spent a year in the city jail awaiting trial. He was eventually released when a local group, whose mission it was to exonerate falsely accused defendants, took up his case.

Leading the charge was a young woman, Alyssa, ironically, the dead man's niece. A series of long conversations led to romance. Louisiana offered only bad memories and few opportunities so Kyle and Alyssa decided to give Florida a try. Kyle worked construction and Alyssa served meals at the local diner, and together they earned enough money to rent a small apartment.

Life was good until Kyle broke his back playing a game of basketball one evening after work. The injury led to his first opioid prescription, which in turn led to his first drug addiction. Alyssa wouldn't have any part of it and returned to Louisiana to live with her parents. With nothing left for him in Florida except the reminder of what he had lost, Kyle began hitchhiking up and down the East coast, eventually landing in New York City three years before we'd met him.

"Why did you settle on New York?" I asked him one day. His answer was simple.

"I've lived in twenty cities, and this is the only one that actually does anything to help the homeless."

An hour later we said goodbye to Kyle, promising to return the following day. Three blocks farther south on the corner of Park Avenue and 34th Street, we met two attractive blonde women, Jan, age 32, and Katie, age 26. At first, Joel and I thought they were two friends hanging out on the street together, however, as we got closer, their hands revealed the truth.

Homeless people often appear to have dirty hands even when they've just been washed. The dirt and grime of the city gets under their fingernails and in their cuticles. After years on the street, no amount of washing could make their hands appear clean. Even after the nail salons reopened in August, and I started taking Maggie with me on occasion for a manicure, it was a challenge for the manicurist to get all the dirt out from her cuticles.

We stopped and offered Jan and Katie sandwiches, which they ate quickly. We exchanged introductions and they told us their nearly identical stories. Both had been living with boyfriends who'd become abusive after losing their jobs as a result of the shutdown. I'd read that domestic abuse had skyrocketed since Governor Cuomo's "pause order" began, and now I saw the evidence of it in the tired and frightened faces of these two young women.

Joel and I looked at each other, speechless. This was a new emotional low for us.

I asked them if they had their IDs—something the homeless were always losing—and both produced them.

"Since you both have IDs, you might like to know the grocery stores are hiring right now," I said. "There is a real shortage of workers because so many people are afraid to work outside of their homes." They both seemed interested so I continued. "Maybe you two could walk around and see if you can get hired and then you might be able to afford a room together," I suggested.

The conversation was going well until I made the mistake of trying to be funny, even though I was sort of being serious.

"Or maybe, get a new boyfriend?"

"I never want another boyfriend for the rest of my life." Katie said.

Realizing my error, I retreated. "Yeah, well maybe the grocery store is a safer bet?"

We visited with Katie and Jan for another thirty minutes and then continued on our way. As we approached 30th Street I saw Maggie jump up from the sidewalk and run toward me.

"I did it!" she exclaimed.

"Did what?"

"I called my case worker."

"And?"

"She got me into a safe haven room last night. I'm living in The Travelers, on 8th Avenue!"

"How did she find a room so quickly?" I asked. "I thought that took months."

"Because Rick was beating me again." I remembered that women who were in danger of abuse held a high priority for the safe haven rooms.

"Wow! Well, bad reason, but great result!" I said. "How long do you have it?"

"Indefinitely!" she exclaimed. "I also called my husband."

"And?"

"He said he was going to his cousin's house on Staten Island tomorrow, and I should come for a visit. He said he'd bring the kids and we could take a ferry ride together!"

"Wow, that's awesome! Here's some money for transportation," I said, handing her twenty dollars. It was the first time I'd given out more than a few dollars to anyone, but I knew Maggie would need money to get to and from Staten Island on her own.

Our next stop was the telephone booths to see Bob and Cathy. We had more clothes for them. Cathy also had a present for us—a large bag of supplies she'd gotten from Bellevue. The bag was so full of socks, toothbrushes, toothpaste, mouthwash and other toiletries that Joel could barely carry it. Over the next several weeks the bag would grow empty as we passed out the necessities to other homeless people.

We handed each of them a sandwich. Cathy took it out of the brown paper bag, unwrapped it and made a face.

"Can you make me a tuna fish sandwich instead of a peanut butter one, please?"

"You think you're ordering from a restaurant?" Bob snipped, shooting her a disgusted look.

"It's okay," I said. "I can make a tuna fish sandwich for her."

Two days later, I saw Maggie. I brought copies of the two books I'd written, having learned that she loved to read. William was there and when he saw the copy of *Unblinded*, he asked if he could look at it. As he flipped the book over from front to back, and then to the front again, a look of amazement appeared on his handsome face.

"I saw someone reading this book in prison!" he shouted, clearly not concerned that we now knew he'd spent time in jail.

"Are you sure you saw someone reading this book?"

"Definitely. I remember because of the dog on the cover. I love labs!" Even though we'd recently donated hundreds of books to prisons and treatment centers, I was still surprised to be standing on Park Avenue talking to an ex-con who'd seen someone reading a book I'd written.

"That's really amazing," I said. "Talk about a small world."

"Yeah, it can be," William said. I turned my attention to Maggie.

"How was your trip to Staten Island?"

"It was good. My husband was impressed with how I looked," she said with a satisfied smirk. "He didn't bring the kids, though. He said he wanted to check me out first to make sure I wouldn't scare them."

"What was the verdict?"

Maggie smiled. "He's bringing them to Staten Island tomorrow!" she shouted gleefully.

I reached into my pocket and handed her forty dollars. "Go buy yourself a new outfit at Target"—one of the few places that sold clothes that was open—"and the rest of the money is for transportation." Rick saw me handing Maggie money, frowned and took off down the street.

"I guess Rick is not thrilled that you've been in contact with your husband?"

"He doesn't know."

"Where does he think you went the other day?"

"I told him I went to visit my sister who lives on Staten Island."

"You have a sister?"

"Yes. She's three years younger than me and has a young son." This was the first I'd heard about a sister. I now knew that Maggie had parents in Florida, a husband and two children who lived two hours away in New Jersey and a sister who lived less than forty-five minutes from where we stood. My gut started nagging me. Something felt wrong.

"How come your family isn't helping you?" I asked.

"It's a long, ugly story," she claimed.

I changed the subject and revisited the job issue. "Do you want to try to get a job now that you have a room and can shower every morning? Maybe in one of the daycares? You have that experience as the head of the nursery school."

"Yeah, that's a good idea. I do have that old resume that I told you about."

"Email it to me, and I'll work on it later today when I go to the office," I offered.

"I will," she promised for a second time. She never did.

As we were about to leave, Henry showed up.

"Got any more sandwiches?" he asked. "I'm starving. I can't make no money panhandling," he complained.

"Everyone is telling us that," I said, handing him a few dollars.

"I need to make some money so I can buy some drugs."

We were flabbergasted that Henry made no attempt to hide his drug use from us. We've gone through The Looking Glass, I thought.

We continued downtown to check on Bob, Cathy, and Tony. Their phone booths were empty, and there was not a trace of any of their belongings.

"Where's all their stuff?" I asked Joel.

"Beats me. This can't be good." I noticed I was worried, as well as surprised. I'd come to be very fond of all of them—Bob's funny stories,

Cathy's childlike innocence, Tony's arms and legs always flailing in every direction whenever we saw him walking down the street.

We continued to the Union Square Market and passed by a young man sitting on the corner. We handed him a sandwich.

"Do you have a home?" he asked in a child-like voice.

"Yes," Joel said.

"Can you take me home with you?"

"No, I'm sorry," said Joel. "We can't do that." The simplicity and innocence of his question left me further unsettled.

"I don't want to go to the market today," I said. "Can we just go home?" Joel agreed, also clearly shaken.

The next day Kyle was not on his corner, and Jan and Katie had disappeared. We never saw them again. I wondered if they got jobs or just changed locations.

When we arrived at Maggie and Rick's corner, some of their friends were waiting for us again. Wayne, Michael, Henry, William, and two women we had never seen before. After handing out the food, I pulled Maggie aside.

"How did the visit with the kids go?" I asked.

Maggie began talking fast, her eyes darting up and down the street. Again, I felt my gut nagging me. Instead of answering my question, she asked a non sequitur.

"Can you send my mom copies of your books?"

"Sure, what's her address?"

Maggie took my phone and added her mom's name and address into my contacts. I held my breath as she entered the information. On several occasions, I'd unsuccessfully tried to get Maggie mother's cell phone number.

Later that afternoon, I went home, grabbed the books and mailed them from the UPS store on my way to work. I included a note to her mother explaining that Maggie had asked me to mail the books and that

I was happy to make contact with her. I put my email and phone number at the bottom of my note.

A few days later, I received a notice that the package had been delivered. I hoped Maggie's mother would reach out to me. It was my first contact with any of her relatives, and it would prove to be one that Maggie would soon regret.

Over the next few weeks Maggie battled with her conflicting desires to be with Rick and to stay safe. She compromised by sleeping in her room every night and returning to the street corner each morning. The effect on Rick was apparent. When we'd first met him, Rick was jovial, funny, and grateful for our daily visits and handouts. Now, he seemed withdrawn and depressed.

"What's wrong with Rick?" I asked Maggie during one of our daily visits. "He always used to be in a good mood."

"He thinks I'm cheating on him when I leave at night."

"To go sleep in your safe haven room?"

"Yeah, he's an idiot."

"Well, he certainly isn't a happy camper," I said, stating the obvious.

"Yeah, and he's drinking a lot too," Maggie added.

The next day Rick confided in Joel that he'd been hitting Maggie. Joel listened but was direct in his advice.

"First, you have to stop hitting her. Then, you need to ask for forgiveness. And last, you need to forgive yourself." Rick's reply was uncharacteristically religious.

"Only God can forgive sins."

Rick was not in sight when we got to his corner on the morning of May 13th. Despite the sunshine, it was cold.

"Where's Rick?" I asked Maggie.

"He went to buy vodka," she admitted.

"Poor guy. Can't you convince him to get some help?"

"Not now," she replied. "He barely speaks to me."

An uneasy feeling of guilt swept through me. Was it my fault that Rick was upset and drinking heavily? Did my friendship with Maggie give her the strength to ask her case worker for a safe haven room, leaving Rick alone on the street at night? I distracted myself from my uncomfortable thoughts by turning my attention to the mundane.

"Well, let's get those shoes you need," I suggested in an effort to change the subject. I opened the Amazon app on my iPhone, typed in "women's shoes" and handed the phone to Maggie.

"Pick whatever pair you want," I offered.

"Can you buy me some tampons instead of shoes?"

"You don't have any tampons?" I asked in disbelief.

"No, and my period is coming. My lowest point as a homeless woman was the morning I woke up in a pool of my monthly blood and I don't want to do that again."

"We can go get some tampons at the drug store in a minute," I offered. "First, let's get you some shoes." Maggie's gray suede winter boots were falling apart and, in any event, were not useful in the spring and summer. I handed her my iPhone and told her to buy what she needed. She stood still, staring at the screen. "Pick out a pair of shoes," I encouraged her.

"I can't," she admitted. "I haven't had to choose anything to wear for three years."

"What type do you want—tennis shoes, slip-ons?" I asked in an effort to prod her to decide.

"I don't know. Can you pick for me?"

I took the phone back and scrolled through the options. I found a nice-looking pair of slip-ons that were a hybrid between a tennis shoe and a flat. I thought they'd be good for the spring weather and even into summer.

"How about these?" I asked, showing her the phone's screen.

"Yeah, they're good," she said, barely glancing at the selections.

"What color do you want? They have pink, black, or white."

"Oh, I love pink! Can I have pink?" Maggie said, now interested in the shoes.

"Sure, no problem. Size six, right?"

"Right, I have small feet."

I hit the *Buy* button. "Done! It says they'll arrive next week."

"I'm so excited. I haven't had a pair of pink shoes since I was a little girl," she said with uncharacteristic joy. "Why so long until they arrive?"

"The mail is all messed up because of COVID." The delayed mail was another effect of the pandemic. We received mail only once or twice a week. Amazon packages that normally arrived on our doorstep within a day or two of placing the order could take over a week now. "Do you need any pants or T-shirts?" I asked, looking down at the torn, dirty pair of sweatpants Maggie wore day in and day out. "Maybe some jeans?"

"Really? You'd buy me a pair of jeans?"

"Sure, how about a pair of Levi's? They hold up really well."

"What size?" I asked.

"The smallest size they have."

I bought a few T-shirts too. Maggie was short, barely five feet tall, and very slight.

"How much do you weigh?" I asked.

"I don't know, actually. It's been a long time since I was on a scale. The last time I was in the hospital I weighed ninety-two pounds."

"Have you always been so thin?"

"Actually, I used to be 250 pounds."

"No way!"

"Yeah. Hold on, I have a picture." Maggie unzipped her bag and pulled out her phone. The picture she showed me was clearly her, yet the woman in the photo bore very little resemblance to the one standing before me that morning. I was surprised, not only by her diminished size, but also by her diminished hair. In the picture, Maggie had long, curly hair that stretched down to her waist. All that appeared under her stocking cap that morning were a few strands of mousy brown, uneven locks.

"Why did you cut your hair?" I asked, shocked by the transformation.

"I didn't. I had to shave my head a few months ago because I got lice."

"Oy, no bueno," I said. "Several other homeless people have told me the same thing."

What I also noticed that morning but didn't have the nerve to ask her about, were her missing teeth. Did Rick knock them out during one of his beatings?

Suddenly, out of nowhere, Rick appeared, running down the middle of 30th Street from the east side. As soon as he saw us talking with Maggie, he started shouting and brandishing a pipe over his head.

"I don't want your peanut butter sandwich or your money!"

Joel and I ran down Park Avenue, stopping a block south. Maggie, on the other hand, didn't budge. She looked directly at Rick with a penetrating stare, expressing a combination of "I can't believe you're acting this way" and "I can't believe what a jerk you are." Even from a block away, I heard Rick scream.

"What are you looking at?"

"I'm looking at a jerk," Maggie yelled.

Maggie caught up with us a few minutes later. While she might have been scared, she was more clearly pissed. "I'm going home to New Jersey to see my kids."

"Great," I said, "and please don't come back."

I was sorry to see her leave, as I'd developed quite a fondness for her over the previous few months. But I knew she was not safe, and it had been almost three years since she'd seen her children.

"Can I have a hug before I go?" she asked.

I hesitated. In the eight weeks of our daily rounds, other than the elbow-bump "handshake" or the occasional brushing of hands as we handed out money, neither Joel nor I had touched a single homeless person. I didn't want to hug her; I also didn't want to reject her.

In the few seconds of awkward silence, Maggie stared at me, her arms at her sides, ready for our first embrace. I stood still, my mind unsuccessfully searching for an excuse for declining a hug. Even though Maggie's body was clean, as she was now starting her days with hot showers, her old winter coat was dirty. It smelled bad—a combination of rotten food and sweat—even from a few feet away. The idea of being enveloped by it was disgusting to me. Still, unable to formulate a reason not to, I hugged her—a long, full frontal, plastered-in-my-arms hug that felt like it would never end. Maggie showed no signs of letting go, so after several seconds, I gently released my arms and, with what I hoped was an imperceptible nudge, separated us.

"I love you," she said, for the first time.

"I love you too," I replied. And I meant it

Nevertheless, I felt dirty and vulnerable to catching the virus. I also felt stupid for never thinking to ask Maggie or anyone else if they were sick. I quelled the rising distaste in my mouth by telling myself I could take a shower when I got home.

"Goodbye," she whispered.

"Good luck, Maggie!"

She turned around and continued running south down Park Avenue. Joel and I headed to Lexington Avenue and back uptown to our apartment, lugging our bag of undistributed sandwiches and granola bars. After being threatened with Rick's pipe, we were done making rounds that day.

When I got home I went directly into the bathroom and washed my face and hands for several minutes. As I dried my face, I stared in the mirror. I told myself to get into the shower or at least change my clothes. But I didn't.

At that point, I was fighting the virus in any way I could. One of those ways was to subdue my own fear. So instead of taking a shower, I went to the office. The entire afternoon, however, I kept my distance from Peter. Even though Peter suspected that he, too, might have had the virus in January, he'd not had an antibody test to confirm it. I was not taking any chances with him due to his age and previous cancer battle. He eventually noticed my side-stepping routine.

"Why are you acting so weird today?"

"I don't want to get within ten feet of you because I hugged Maggie this morning?"

"Why would you do that?"

"There was this incident with Rick and then we all ran away. She was going home and wanted a hug before she left."

"You're nuts," Peter said.

I had to agree with him. I went into the bathroom and washed my hands and face again for good measure.

The next morning I saw Maggie right back on the corner taking a nap with Rick, snuggled in his arms. I stood a few feet from her and watched in disbelief as she lay unaware of my gaze. *Did she even go to New Jersey? Was the whole thing just a con to get money from me?*

Suddenly, Maggie jumped up and before I could utter a word, she started explaining that while she had gone to New Jersey, she and her husband were still working out the details of her permanent return.

"He said I could live in his father's old house as long as I took over the job of home-schooling the kids."

"So when are you going home for good?" I asked, with a bit of an edge to my voice.

"Soon."

"Soon doesn't really mean anything, Maggie. You need to set a date."

Maggie nodded, yet said nothing.

The following week, Maggie told me the truth, which I had already come to suspect.

"Tray, I never went home. Not once. Not ever. Everything I've told you about going home and speaking to my husband was a lie."

"Why can't you go home?"

"I just can't." I pressed her for more details. She changed the subject.

It would be a long time before I could string together the pieces of a very complex web of half-truths.

■ – ■ – ■

MAGGIE WRIGHT, MAY 2020

The first thing I noticed was the sound. It was a typical New York City morning. After three years of waking up on the sidewalk, I'd grown accustomed to certain things. The sound of the garbage truck is what roused me from my slumber, the loud beeping, unforgiving so early in the morning. The next thing I heard was the sound of the construction workers greeting each other. How could they sound so jolly this morning?

I finally got the courage to open my eyes. Once my gaze focused on the sky, I knew it was not yet 7:00 a.m. Yet another "perk" of homelessness. I could tell what time it was by the color of the sky and the shadows. My suspicions were confirmed when I saw the seagulls pass by overhead—a pair, they always came to search for scraps, far from home, before the clock hit 7:00 a.m.

I closed my eyes again and tried to remember what a spring morning in New York City smelled like. A mixture of yesterday's trash yet to be picked up. Morning dew on the few trees that stood on Park Avenue and 30th Street. The smell of coffee and bacon wafting over from the cart parked on the corner across the street. But there was no cart that morning—we were in the middle of a pandemic.

Absentmindedly, I reached up and touched the side of my face. A familiar feeling awaited me. A bruise—a bad one this time. I would definitely have a black eye. Another day of explanations. I was sure Traci would notice. I started making up my excuse. As I got up from my bed on the sidewalk, my whole body ached. I felt much older than my thirty-eight years.

The last, and final, thing I noticed was the taste in my mouth. Ironic, since I had not tasted anything in almost three years since I'd fallen backward onto the sidewalk. My tongue still responded to stimuli, however, and this morning, all I could "taste" was an overwhelming sense of salt and brine—blood.

As I got up from my makeshift bed, exhausted, sore and defeated, the remembered taste of blood in my mouth, I made the decision that would forever change my life. No more beatings. No more mornings waking up on the sidewalk conquered. Last night would be the last.

At 9:00 a.m. sharp, I told Rick I was going to use the bathroom at McDonald's. I had saved the two dollars Traci had given me the day before to buy a cup of coffee. Instead, even before relieving myself, I headed directly to the LinkedIn phone across the street.

After three rings, she answered.

"Hello, Lina? I'm ready."

CHAPTER 7

The Longest Night

———■———

The phone rang in the middle of the night, and even before I heard his voice on the speaker, I knew something was wrong.

"Dad, can you and Mom come to my apartment? I'm really sick."

"We're on our way," Joel replied.

In less than a minute, we were dressed and out the door. We ran the three blocks to Chad's apartment.

We found him in bed in a fetal position. Within a few minutes of our arrival he started to vomit. The next few hours were a continuous loop of vomiting, crawling back into bed and enduring the pain that pulsated in his upper chest area. He insisted I stay by his side, my first clue that something was terribly wrong.

We thought he had food poisoning. The takeout containers sat empty on his kitchen counters. He thought he had a hernia.

We'd soon find out we were all wrong.

No one wanted to go near a hospital during the pandemic. After five hours of hoping Chad would stop vomiting, however, it was clear we had no choice but to call 911. As they loaded him into the ambulance and drove away, all I could think was please God, not again.

■ – ■ – ■

February 2018. Chad and his cousin Collin came to visit us in Turks. On their last day, they decided to watch the opening ceremony of the Winter Olympics at a local sports bar in town. They decided to walk, knowing they'd be drinking.

They never returned.

When the phone rang at 6 a.m., I considered not answering it, as if my denial might shield me from the inevitable reality. Five rings later, my instinct to hide gave way to my need to know who was on the phone, in the hope they had news of Chad and Collin.

Collin's wife, Dee, was calling from New York. She was crying.

"Collin and Chad have been in a serious car accident." My mind tried to process the information. How could they have been in a car accident when they walked to town?

"Where are they now?"

"At the Cheshire Medical Center."

I woke Joel.

"Chad and Collin have been in a car accident."

"Where are they?" he asked as he slipped his tee shirt over his head.

"Cheshire Medical Center."

Joel bolted out the door. Twenty minutes later, he called. "Chad needs emergency surgery. The doctor has cleared the operating schedule for the morning. They're taking him into the operating room now."

"What happened?"

"The boys got a ride home with one of the guests staying here at the hotel. He lost control of the car and hit that brick wall by the grocery store."

"Weren't they wearing their seatbelts?"

"Yes, and Chad's nearly cut him in half upon impact."

Cheshire Medical Center had two surgeons on staff, one from Zimbabwe, the other from Jamaica. They were both needed in the operating room. In the operating theater, Chad's intestines were examined inch by inch, pressed between the doctor's thumb and forefinger—an operation referred to as "running the intestines." With no fancy cameras or laparoscopic operating tools, the only way to put Chad back together was to run the entire length of his intestines through the surgeon's hands, looking for areas that needed repair or removal.

Three feet of Chad's intestines were too badly damaged to be repaired and were removed. Three hours into surgery, the doctors prepared to close him up when they noticed that Chad's hip tendon was torn off the bone. Another hour of surgery ensued.

Five hours later, Chad was wheeled from the operating room to the intensive care unit. He was the only patient there. Joel was allowed to see him for a few minutes. Chad was unresponsive. Drains, breathing devices, and catheters emerged from various parts of his body. Incessant beeping alerted the nurses to his blood pressure, temperature and oxygen levels, unnerving Joel even more than when the surgery had begun.

Three weeks after he was wheeled into the emergency room, Chad walked out of the Cheshire Medical Center, having lost three feet of his intestine and having gained a large hernia on his side that would need to be repaired once he recovered.

But Chad was alive.

Three years later, Chad was now in the hospital again, in the middle of New York City, in the middle of the pandemic. The three feet of intestine Chad lost in Turks was a critical three feet—the section where bile is reabsorbed before waste material descends into the lower bowel. This loss had caused the formation of gallstones and a large one was blocking the duct to his pancreas, resulting in an acute case of pancreatitis. Emergency surgery was scheduled to remove the stone.

In order to keep ourselves calm, Joel and I made our morning rounds despite having been up all night. Maggie couldn't believe we were on the streets handing out sandwiches. She seemed to get it, however, when I said I wasn't going home until the hospital called and said Chad was out of surgery.

"I'd be going crazy if one of my kids was on the operating table today. I totally understand why you're trying to keep yourself distracted."

No one from the hospital ever called. By dinner time, I comforted myself with the thought that if Chad had died on the operating table that morning, someone would have surely called us by now. Finally, ten hours after his surgery began, my cell phone rang. It flew out of my hands as I tried to answer it.

"Hi, Mom. I'm back in my room."

"How do you feel?"

Chad's response was typical.

"Not bad."

"When are they releasing you?"

"I don't know, Mom. I'm tired. I need to go back to sleep."

I fell asleep that night grateful that Chad was alive but with a nagging feeling that his current crisis was not over.

The next morning Maggie called in a panic. "I'm so sorry to bother you. I know you have your hands full with Chad, but I need you!"

"What's happened now?"

"Rick's been arrested. The police took him to jail."

"What did he do this time?"

"He hit a man with a pipe." I wondered if it was the same pipe we'd seen him brandishing at us the day we ran down Park Avenue. Bail was set at $1,000 and a court date for the middle of June.

Maggie had no way of raising that kind of money, and although she was afraid of being alone, she was not eager to have Rick back on the street hitting her. Even his mother had very little to say and no money to offer to make bail when Maggie called to tell her that her son was in jail again.

"He's better off in jail than on the street—go enjoy yourself for a change," his mother said and hung up.

The following night William, the charismatic Black man who often hung out on her corner, invited Maggie to dinner—a picnic he prepared. They sat by the East River and before the night was over William had quite literally charmed the pants off of her.

When I ran into William the next day he had a big smile on his face and couldn't wait to tell me the news.

"I sure hope Rick doesn't get out of jail any time soon because I'm afraid Maggie will go right back to him," I said.

"That won't happen," he assured me with a twinkle in his eye. "That was made certain last night."

When I saw Maggie later that day, I winked and said, "Heard you had a good time last night."

"I sure did, Tray. And it was so nice to have someone treat me well for a change."

William had more good news to share. His permanent housing assignment was imminent. The only obstacle between William and his new home was a requirement that he quarantine for fourteen days in his safe haven room to ensure he did not have the virus. Joel urged him to agree to the quarantine and get it over with. After spending so many years in jail, however, William just couldn't do it.

"I just can't be locked up again," he admitted. "No matter what the cost. I've been in and out of prison or juvenile detention centers since I was thirteen."

Rebellious by nature, William could not follow rules even as a child. He started his lifelong tendency to steal by helping himself to candy and soda pop at the bodegas in his neighborhood. As he grew, so did his infractions. Candy turned into beer, which eventually led to cash to buy drugs. But it wasn't until his mother suddenly died from an asthma attack when he was a teenager that things really went downhill.

His father had died the year before, and William was convinced that his mother's new boyfriend had hidden her inhaler. At her funeral, William tried to take his mother's body out of the casket. He was restrained and then hospitalized. It was the beginning of a long descent into darkness that would transcend far more than the numerous prison cells he would encounter.

Four years before we'd met him, William had come to New York City from New Jersey on a whim. "I just heard an inner voice telling me to come here. I had nothing left in New Jersey, and I thought a new place would help break the endless cycle of incarcerations and releases," he said.

When he'd arrived in New York, he set up a makeshift home on 32nd Street atop a subway grate that blew hot air in the winter and cool air in the summer. The following year, William was placed in a series of safe haven rooms, none of which worked out because he could not get along with his roommates.

Discouraged, he registered with a different agency. His first placement with them was likewise a failure. For the next six months he slept in a series of bank vestibules and on the subway. During the day, he roamed Midtown and met Maggie and Rick. By the time we'd met him, however, he was living in a safe haven room with a roommate he liked.

Making it even more difficult to comply with the fourteen-day quarantine requirement, William believed he didn't have the virus because he'd already contracted it in March, probably from Maggie as they shared blunts. She'd recently told me that she'd been so sick in early March she never got up off the sidewalk for two days. Other than a violent stomach ache that lasted twenty-four hours and landed him in the ER, William had been asymptomatic. But he tested positive so he was absolutely sure he'd had the virus just two months prior.

As coveted as a safe haven room was, being assigned low-income, permanent housing was akin to winning the lottery in the homeless community. It also represented a first step toward meaningful reintegration into society. With shelter and utilities provided, and food stamps available to cover basic nutritional needs, the next step was finding employment. William was so close, yet the quarantine issue stood in his way. No amount of Joel's urging would change William's mind.

"Do you have a better plan?" Joel asked.

William winked, and I could tell he did, in fact, have a plan. "I have an idea up my sleeve," he boasted.

Early Thursday morning Chad called with the news I'd been expecting. He was scheduled to have his gallbladder removed at eight a.m. At ten o'clock the phone rang again. I jumped up from the couch hoping it was the doctor calling with the news that Chad was out of surgery.

"The surgery is off," Chad said.

"Why?"

"I'm too sick to have more surgery today."

"What do you mean you're too sick?"

"My blood count numbers are not good." Feelings of dread and relief battled for control of my emotions. At least, Chad would not be on another operating table that day. I was only slightly comforted by this thought. His gallbladder could produce another stone at any moment and irreparably injure his already damaged pancreas, a vital organ he could not live without. And it had to come out at some point, so the sooner the better.

On the evening of Saturday, May 23rd, five days after the ambulance had arrived to take Chad to the hospital, he called from his hospital bed. We were upstate visiting Kyra.

"They said I could go home," he announced with a tone I was unable to decipher. "They can't take the gall bladder out for another month."

"We're in Mahopac, but we'll come right back to the city. I'll call you when we pull up in front of the hospital."

Joel looked over at me as I hung up the phone. "We're leaving?"

"Chad is being released. We have to pick him up."

"But we're just about to have dinner," Joel said.

"Can you pack it up for the ride?" I asked.

We gathered our things, said our goodbyes and left. As we got into the car, I looked over my shoulder at Kyra standing on the front porch.

Our eyes met. In a moment of self-pity, I felt sorry for us. It had been a long two years since Chad's accident in Turks.

The roads and highways were still empty, so we made it to the city in less than an hour. As we pulled up in front of the hospital, my stomach cramped. I was expecting to see Chad accompanied to the front door in a wheelchair. Instead, I saw him walking through the empty lobby, dazed and confused, resembling a soldier who'd come home from war. Nevertheless, despite his bedraggled and noticeably thinner appearance, the event felt more like we were picking him up from the movies when he was a teenager. I jumped out of the car, helped Chad into the front seat and got into the back. He was unusually quiet.

"What's wrong? Are you in a lot of pain?" I asked.

"They told me I could go home. Then they made me sign a paper saying I was leaving against medical advice," he said. I chalked it up to yet another effect of the virus. Everyone seemed confused since the pandemic had started.

We took Chad back to our apartment. He ate some soup and recounted his last five days in the hospital. Two things he told us were confusing. The first was that the nurses did not wear masks at the nursing station. The second was that when he'd asked them about it, they said that there had not been a single case of the virus inside the hospital since the beginning of May. I wondered where all the virus victims were.

I slept little that night—one ear open in case Chad called out for help, the other open, too, in case my first ear didn't hear him. I thought about what it must be like for the mothers of the homeless people sleeping on the street that night. Did they wonder whether their children were safe? Were they calling out for their mothers in their sleep?

Despite Chad's bad luck in needing to be hospitalized during the pandemic, I felt lucky that night. I knew where he was sleeping. I knew he was alive. And I knew that if he called out for me, I'd hear him.

Despite our own personal struggles, on May 24th there was reason to hope. The city reported the lowest virus statistics since the daily tally had begun—479 new cases; 119 new hospitalizations and 49 deaths. We were now more than seven weeks past the first peak, with no significant upticks. After weeks of declining numbers, there were very few people who did not agree the virus was on the decline. Nevertheless, people were still afraid of a second wave. It almost seemed as if a significant number of New Yorkers did not *want* to believe the city was no longer in the grave danger it once was.

The next morning, we ran into Mark, the man from Connecticut, on Park Avenue. He reported matter-of-factly, as he had boldly declared the last time we'd seen him, that he had indeed found both a job and an apartment.

"That's just great news!" Joel said.

"And I've been off crack for a month!" he added with pride.

Crack is a free base form of cocaine that can be smoked, offering a short, intense high. Maggie explained to us that crack was the poor man's form of cocaine that is smoked rather than snorted. "The rich man snorts cocaine; the poor guy smokes it," she said on more than one occasion. Crack came in the form of a crystal rock that was smoked in a pipe.

It is also the most addictive form of the drug and, ironically, not inexpensive, costing over twenty dollars for a high that does not last very long. Maggie, who had once been an opioid abuser and still liked her vodka, could never understand why people would pay so much for so little.

"It's the biggest waste," she'd exclaim whenever the subject came up. "It's literally like burning money."

We'd also heard about K2, a synthetic form of marijuana smoked in a rolled cigarette-type joint called a blunt. Unlike pot, however, K2 can have serious side effects such as rapid heart rate, vomiting, agitation, and hallucinations. The most widely-used forms among the homeless people we knew were called Cotton Ball and Spice. The most potent blunt was a mixture of crack cocaine and K2, called a Woolie.

"Even without the crack, the K2 alone is like weed on steroids," Maggie told us.

K2 products are made from dried plants sprayed with mind-altering chemicals, created by scientists to be used in research. The effects of taking a hit are felt within seconds and can last for up to six hours.

Mark was right to be proud that morning. He was the first homeless person we knew who had gotten himself off the street, found a job and become clean.

"How'd you get a job?" Joel asked.

"A man who lives on 31st Street helped me. I'm working part-time in the Bronx."

"That's just great! What are you doing?"

"I'm a custodian in one of the city's nonprofit agencies that prepares food for the homeless."

"Wow, talk about life coming full circle," Joel said. "Now you are helping the homeless!"

Mark's part-time job turned into a full-time position two weeks later. A week after that, he was supervising six people. He'd found a room in Harlem for $175 per week.

The transformation was nothing short of a miracle. When we'd first met Mark he was homeless, bearded and hooded. That morning he was sheltered, shaved, and employed. He now looked like someone who had grown up in a good home in an affluent suburb of Connecticut.

Not everyone was doing as well as Mark, however. Kyle reported a strange pain in his side that sounded ominously similar to the one Chad had described the day he'd gone to the ER. He also reported visual and auditory hallucinations that were very real to him.

"They look like gargoyles coming out of the buildings," he said, describing their appearance. "And they yell and curse at me."

"What exactly are they saying?" I asked, alarmed.

"I don't want to say," Kyle replied.

While sympathetic to his hallucinations, I was more immediately concerned about his description of the pain in his side.

"It's probably nothing, but that pain sounds a lot like what Chad described the night he went to the hospital. You better get it checked out if it doesn't go away soon," I advised.

"Yes, Mom," he joked.

"Come on, Mr. Funny Man. I'm serious."

"Okay, okay," he said. It was no joke to me. I'd started to feel like a mother—or at least an aunt—and I didn't want to see anything happen to Kyle. To my shock, as I stood on the street looking at him, I realized I loved him. I liked all of the homeless people we'd met, even Rick, despite his numerous violent outbursts. But I definitely loved Maggie and Kyle. Not another one, I thought. *What is happening to me?*

"Just when you thought you were free of your parents," I said lightheartedly, "you end up with a replacement." Kyle broke out into a belly laugh.

"That's okay with me," he said. "You guys are the parents I never had. And Chad is always so nice to me too."

At that point, Chad had joined our efforts to help the homeless and made our morning rounds for us whenever we were not in the city. In doing so, he'd become good friends with not only Kyle, but also Maggie and William. He was also very fond of Bob, Cathy and Tony.

I noticed Kyle wasn't wearing his green jacket. His arms were exposed, and I saw needle marks. My heart sank. I had suspected Kyle was using heroin to control his back pain, but I'd never had the courage to ask him about it outright. I knew enough about opioid addiction from a friend who'd lost her only son to it. His first athletic injury led to his first opioid prescription and, eventually, to heroin when his doctor would no longer give him a prescription for more opioids. He was dead before his 21st birthday. I knew too many parents with children who struggled with addictions. It rarely ended in a good way.

We said our goodbyes and continued walking down Park Avenue to check on the others. I broached the subject with Joel.

"I saw needle marks on Kyle's arms."

"I know, Trace, I didn't want to tell you."

"Can't he get a prescription for Suboxone to control his back pain?"

"Not if he's a heroin addict. He'd have to detox first."

"Can't he do that?"

"He said he needs his Medicaid card first so he can go into treatment."

"Why doesn't he have that?"

"I don't know, but his case worker is working on it."

"Everything is always hurry up and wait for the homeless. I don't get it. Can't we do better for them?"

"I'm sure Karen is doing the best she can," Joel said.

Neither Bob nor Cathy were doing well that morning either. They both had reappeared in their telephone booths. Bob reported that he'd been in the hospital yet again, unable to breathe. Cathy, depressed, had gone to hang out in a park. We were worried Bob had finally caught the virus. Nevertheless, his sixth COVID test was negative. Rather, the reason for his breathing difficulty was potentially even more dire—fluid in his lungs. The doctors were unsure of the cause.

I was surprised that Bob kept testing negative. In fact, not a single one of the homeless people we knew had, to our knowledge, contracted the virus during the time we'd been making our rounds, even though we knew that both Maggie and William had had it in early March. This seemed inconceivable given the fact that they shared cigarettes, drinks and blunts, not to mention their living conditions on the streets.

While the homeless people we knew did not appear to be unusually susceptible to the virus, they did seem to be prey to frequent robberies. We could not figure out whether they were stealing from one another or whether strangers were stealing from them as they slept. In either event, they were easy targets.

In addition to being robbed regularly, they were constantly losing things. They seemed unable to hold on to anything for long except what was literally on their bodies—and sometimes not even that. We'd already bought numerous tee shirts for each of them.

If anyone was lucky enough to get a cell phone, it was often stolen or lost within a week. Maggie was already on her third phone since we'd met her. Likewise, any spare clothes and even their blankets disappeared.

The most problematic loss, however, was an ID card, which is why I was so surprised when both Jan and Katie, the two young women we'd met on Park Avenue the month before, had theirs. Without an ID, the homeless could not get Medicaid, food stamps, etc.

By the end of May, we were forced to face an unpleasant truth—the hundreds of dollars we'd spent and the countless hours we'd invested had not substantially changed the circumstances of our homeless friends. Feelings of helplessness and frustration began to overwhelm and discourage me.

It's hopeless," I said to Joel one morning. "Nothing we do really makes a difference."

Joel agreed, yet pointed out the obvious question—what were our choices? Quit now or keep showing up and moving forward.

"I'm not giving up until we get each one of them off the street," he declared. "Just look at the difference in Maggie since she got her safe haven room."

I was with him on that one. Despite the frustration, the setbacks, and even the great investment of time and money, I knew Joel was right. Many of the homeless people we'd met had become our friends. I wanted them *all* off the streets. My desire was real. And persistent.

I noticed the transformation in Joel before I felt it in myself. Little by little, we were becoming unblind—unblind to the privileged life we'd enjoyed, unblind to the gross racial and socio-economic inequalities that existed in our society, unblind to the daily suffering of others. So we kept showing up, unable at that point, even if we had wanted, to turn away.

■ – ■ – ■

MAGGIE WRIGHT, MAY 2020

The first time Lina brought me into The Travelers, I was shaking and dizzy. My hands were sweating, despite the cold, and I was unable to speak clearly because my mouth was dry.

I'd been on the streets with Rick for three years. It didn't seem right that I should sleep inside, in a warm bed, while he was out there, shivering on the sidewalk. The fact of the matter, however, was I was only standing in The Travelers' lobby because of his violence. It was a bad situation all around.

The first night I stayed at The Travelers was blissful. I was given a bag with bedding and toiletries. Even though I didn't have any clean clothes, I took a long, hot shower in the communal bathroom and then returned to my assigned room. I laid down on the bed and fell asleep. For the first time in years, I slept through the night.

When I returned to the corner in the morning, Rick was pacing back and forth. I could tell he was upset, even from several blocks away. I approached him cautiously.

"Why did you take a shower? Who were you sleeping with last night?"

I knew right then and there that sleeping at The Travelers, while solving one set of problems, was going to present a whole new set of challenges. Even though I'd been faithful to Rick from our first day together, he was always suspicious, even when I ran an errand at his request.

"Are you out of your mind?" I shouted.

"Enjoying your nightly freedom?" he asked, a malicious sneer distorting his mouth.

As the days passed, his anger and suspicions grew. It soon became clear that it was easier for me to just sleep on the sidewalk with him—the warm bed and good night's sleep were not worth the drama they caused.

Nevertheless, I knew I'd have to go to The Travelers every three days, or I would lose my room. My sacrifice was creating my own anger and resentment toward Rick. He should have been thrilled for me that I had a safe place to sleep. Instead, he made me feel guilty.

To my surprise, quite apart from having to appease Rick, I struggled to show up at The Travelers once every three days. I'd grown accustomed to not having to be anywhere at any given time. This was the reason I never sent Traci my resume even after I could sleep well and shower. There was no way I could work every day.

The freedom that homelessness brings is hard to describe. There are no responsibilities, no bills to pay, no appointments to keep. I didn't realize how much I liked this, and, as incredible as it may sound, I resented having to show up at The Travelers even once every three days to sign in for my room.

Regardless, I did show up. I was not going to lose that room. I'd slipped into a different reality—one where I was safe, warm and no longer hungry. The realization that Rick was not coming with me slowly dawned, terrifying me. I knew I had to make some tough choices. Even though I am not religious, I prayed that I would have the courage to make the right ones.

CHAPTER 8

Absence of Light

■

The summer weather finally arrived just in time for Memorial Day weekend. Chad was feeling better, and his gallbladder surgery was still a few weeks away so we decided to go to Mahopac.

On Saturday afternoon everyone took a nap. I slipped down to the lake to play fetch with the two dogs—our lab and our daughter's Goldendoodle. Despite being in a very different reality, I could not stop thinking about our new homeless friends. It was like I was trying to solve a legal problem, even though I knew it was intractable. *You're not going to come up with any answers that the experts haven't already thought of.* I decided to meditate to still my racing mind.

I closed my eyes and focused my attention on my breath. In. Out. Within a few seconds, I was distracted by thoughts of the homeless. I tried again. Two breaths later, I lost my focus a second time. I tried a mantra. *"I am grateful that Chad is alive."* Three gratefuls later, and I started thinking about work. *This is hopeless. I'll never be able to meditate.*

The water gently undulated as boats passed by. I gazed at the shifting water line near the shore. The in-and-out rhythm mimicked what I'd tried to achieve with my breathing and mantra. My mind was drawn to a single point of focus—the pulsating water as it approached and receded. Everything else, including the two dogs vying for my attention, became blurred and my hearing dulled.

Then it felt like the perimeter of my body melded into the surroundings. For a moment, my mind released its omnipresent connection to the self. "I" no longer seemed an appropriate pronoun to define who or what I thought I was. The water became me, and I it. A deep sense of inner peace replaced what had previously been agitation and frustration.

A few seconds later, however, I sensed a tight knot in my chest. Its edges were distinct, as if it were a tumor or foreign object. I was trying to define its exact location when I was seized by an inexplicable fear. I shook my head and stood up, grabbed the ball and continued playing fetch with the dogs.

I'd started my spiritual practice in 2012 when a neighbor introduced us to a group of lectures called The Pathwork. I wasn't immediately interested, to say the least. I'm analytical by nature and need proof. Math was my favorite subject in school; physics, a close second. I cannot believe in something I cannot see. While I have faith that there is something bigger than me "out there," I also resist abstract concepts. However, as I devoured one Pathwork lecture after the next, reading, outlining, and reading them again, something in my soul that I could not explain, and did not recognize, began to stir. It was the beginning of a transformation that was now being rapidly accelerated by my daily interactions with the homeless.

It was almost an exact mathematical formula. The more I focused on others, the more at peace I was. That was just one part of the transformation. There was something more profound taking place that resembled my experience meditating by the water. The lines between the homeless and myself started to blur. I knew we were distinct physical entities, yet I started to feel an intermingling below the surface of the exterior world that connected us at a fundamental, and far more profound, level.

On Memorial Day, I took my first swim of the season. The lake water was still cold, but I hadn't swum since March when we'd left Turks. The shock of plunging into the cold lake was soon relieved by the joy of swimming through the crystal clear water. Within minutes, I was in a meditative state again, often referred to by athletes as the "zone." Whatever its name, the effect was cleansing.

When I got back to the house, however, the serenity of my first swim in over two months was disrupted the moment I heard the news— George Floyd had been killed by a police officer. Protests started in Minneapolis and quickly spread throughout the U.S. and the world. Many grew worried about a resurgence of the virus as masses of New Yorkers, with little to no social distancing, took to the streets in peaceful protest. Then what we all feared might happen, did, when some other less well-motivated city residents used the protests as an opportunity for looting. Store windows were smashed, robberies began. Even Macy's was burglarized. Maggie was especially worried that William's tendency to steal would become even worse.

"It's hard enough for him to resist the temptation to steal, even in normal circumstances, but when everyone else is doing it, he thinks it is okay. And he can't make much money these days selling K2."

While most of the homeless people we knew smoked K2, much to our disappointment, William sold it. He'd buy a bag for fifty dollars and then walk around the streets selling blunts for five dollars each. This resulted in more than one turf war with ensuing arrests and/or hospitalizations. Maggie was not happy about this but had to agree it was probably better than his other "employment." William also stole cases of Ensure from drug stores. He'd walk in, grab several cases and walk out.

"How does he get away with that?" I asked.

"They're not allowed to touch him, much less detain him. They have to call the police and by the time they arrive, William's long gone."

"That does not sound right. We've come a long way from the days when store owners would tackle customers if they tried to steal. Looks like societal norms have changed quite a bit."

"It's ridiculous," Maggie agreed. "The other day, we walked into a CVS to pick up his prescription and the woman at the register put up her hand and yelled at him."

"What did she say?"

"She said, *please, not today*. She was practically begging him not to take anything."

"That sounds so unfair."

"Yeah, and last week he was walking out with his Ensure when the store manager saw him, called him back into the store and paid for the stuff himself."

"Why would he do that?" I asked.

"He said he was going to lose his job if any more Ensure was stolen."

"We've come too far in protecting the rights of the accused," I said, this time with conviction. While I felt bad William believed his only way of making money was selling drugs or stealing, I was also furious with him for putting himself, and hence Maggie, at risk.

As the weeks and months passed, I would read story after story in the local newspapers about the problem. An increasing number of New Yorkers were caught on video camera walking out of grocery stores with everything from sirloin steaks to rack of lambs.

After several days of looting, trash cans were removed from the street corners to prevent their use in breaking store windows. Suddenly, in addition to shattered windows and shuttered stores, trash was piling up everywhere. It felt like the city's hard-earned progress was set back by months.

New Yorkers are resilient by nature and the trash problem was no exception. Previously-sheltering dwellers, still fearful of the virus, yet now on a mission, emerged to clean up the trash, block by block, day after day, for a week, until the looting subsided and the public trash cans, mercifully, returned.

"I never thought I'd be so happy to see a trash can," I shouted to a nearby policeman as we walked down Park Avenue making our daily morning rounds.

"Yes, we take everything for granted around here until we don't have it anymore," the police officer replied.

I found Maggie waiting for us on her corner. We had decided to try to open a bank account for her at Chase. This seemingly simple task proved challenging. In order to open an account a person needed two forms of identification, one of which must have their photo on it. Maggie had her New York State ID but none of the other accepted types.

"Let's just forget this," she said as her patience wore thin. It was right then I realized that she, and almost all of the homeless people I'd come to know, shared a similar reaction to frustration. They quickly became agitated and wanted to give up.

"We're not going anywhere until we get this account opened for you," I reassured her.

Maggie's case worker, Lina, the best one we'd met that spring, provided a letter on her agency's letterhead confirming Maggie's status as one of its clients. I held my breath as the teller showed the letter to the branch manager.

When the teller returned to our window, I was sure he was going to say he couldn't help us. I was surprised and delighted when he showed Maggie the debit card options and asked her which design she wanted. She squealed in delight and chose one with a *Star Wars* theme.

"Wow," Maggie exclaimed as we left the bank, her newly printed debit card in hand. We almost got hit by a taxi on Park Avenue as we admired her new possession, which entitled her to far more than the fifty dollars we'd deposited into her account.

"I just can't believe it! I have a bank account again." I was grateful that Rick was still in jail. I knew she would give him the money she just deposited if he returned.

A week later, the dire predictions about the virus resurgence proved false as the city's numbers continued to drop, despite the many protests. On Wednesday, June 3rd, the city reported its first day in three months with zero confirmed deaths. As people celebrated the good news, the naysayers continued to predict doom and gloom as a result of the continuing, yet diminished, protests. People were divided again. One side supported the protests and indeed welcomed them. The other side was silently hoping everyone would soon grow tired of the latest *raison d'etre* and go home.

People began voicing their opinions and venting their frustrations on social media. The daily messages of hate grew more rampant as the protests dragged on. Fortunately, there was one thing that united most New Yorkers that June—the planned Phase One reopening of the city scheduled for June 8th. We were all determined to do whatever was necessary to make sure that date was met.

Saturday, June 6th was my sixty-fifth birthday. I'm not prone to looking back, yet that day, I found myself doing just that and wondering how it was possible that I really was on Medicare. I also spent a good portion of the day reflecting on how it was possible that a woman who grew up in the cornfields of Virginia could end up working and living in New York City, only to one day find herself walking the streets, handing out sandwiches to the homeless.

At some level, I knew that the truth about why we were doing our work with the homeless related back to my own personal history, parts of which lay hidden. Most, if not all of it, had to do with the relationship with my mother.

Cornfields—corporate office—New York City streets. Mine had been a long journey.

■ – ■ – ■

June 1955. Before I emerged into the world, shattering one of my mother's vertebras in the process, the course of my life, its inevitable trajectory, and its carefully-guarded secrets were set in motion. Even before that D-day, there was another little girl whose life was also set in motion on a single day, by a single incident—not by a birth, rather, by a death.

It was February 1936, and my grandmother Mary was busy cleaning the last of the pots and pans when she heard the front door close. Her husband, Ralph Tully, left without saying good-bye as was his custom. It was Friday night, and Ralph would be meeting his buddies at the local bar. Ralph was not one to keep his friends waiting.

Mary's eldest, Jean, my mother, was reading to her little brother and sister, Ralph Jr., four, and the baby Mary Joyce, who was still in diapers. Only in second grade, it was already clear that Jean was an exceptional student. Mary held out hope that Jean would one day attend college, although she could not imagine how the tuition would be paid.

When Mary woke up in the middle of the night to relieve herself, her feet almost froze in the few minutes it took her to walk down the hall and use the one bathroom the family shared. Even though they lived in Alexandria, Virginia, it was still cold in the middle of the winter, especially in the middle of the night.

Her husband was not yet home. Mary did not think too much of it and quickly checked on her three children to make sure they were still tucked under their covers. She then returned to the warmth of her bed, pulled the blankets over her head and fell back to sleep.

Mary was awakened by the Saturday morning sunshine streaming through the lace curtains even before her baby's first cries. She reached over to touch Ralph, but his side of the bed was empty. It was clear it had not been slept in. Ralph had been known to stagger in drunk well into the early hours of the morning, but he was always by her side when she woke up.

Mary knew something was wrong.

She warmed the baby's bottle and woke Jean, handing it to her before the little girl had fully opened her eyes.

"Can you feed your sister, please? I'm going to run to the store for some bread and milk."

Jean knew something was wrong. Her mother never ran out of bread and milk. It was delivered twice a week to the front door, week in and week out. In fact, their milkman was so reliable that their supplies would be waiting in the makeshift icebox by their front door, even in the middle of a blizzard.

Despite the bright sunshine of the morning, it had snowed overnight. Still in her pajamas, Mary stepped into her black rubber boots without kicking off her slippers and threw her grey wool coat over her faded, yellow-flowered, nightgown. Jean arrived in the living room with the baby on her hip in time to see her mother fly out the front door.

"I'll be right back," Mary called out as she ran down the front steps of their house on Luray Avenue. Mary turned left and marched in the direction of the local bar. Her journey ended less than fifty feet from her driveway, when she saw Ralph, asleep in a snow bank. A red-haired Irish woman with a hot temper to match, Mary was planning her tongue-lashing speech as she approached her husband.

"What do you think you're doing sleeping out here?"

Ralph did not wake up. Mary bent down and gave him a good shake. Other than a faint grunt, he did not respond. Mary ran across the street and started banging on her neighbors' front door, waking every dog on the block. Soon, both the husband and wife appeared, dazed and confused, still in their pajamas, only to witness Mary talking nonsense and frantically pointing to Ralph who was passed out in the snow across the street.

It took all three of them to drag his weight down the street and up the front stoop, not to mention the staircase inside. Twenty minutes later, Mary and her neighbors had Ralph back in his bed.

The help was too little, too late. The next morning, Ralph died from pneumonia. My grandmother was suddenly a widow with three young children, no job, very little money and a broken heart. My mother, Jean, was fatherless.

Two years later, Mary remarried William McCormick, whose claim to fame was that his grandfather Cyrus invented the reaper. My step-grandfather kept a copy of the patent in his basement. I often wondered whether my grandmother remarried for love or financial necessity. Perhaps it was a little of both.

While she might have escaped poverty by remarrying, Mary did not escape the bottle. McCormick was also an alcoholic. My mother grew up in a home filled with all the lies and deceits that accompany an alcoholic's life. By the time she went to college on a basketball scholarship at George Washington University, fulfilling her mother's dream of her first-born receiving a higher education, her stepfather had joined AA and never drank another drop. Nevertheless, the damage was done.

Despite her tumultuous childhood, my mother flourished. A natural beauty, gifted athlete, and scholar, she played four years of basketball while earning her degree. She met my father, Charles Eugene Medford, on a blind date in 1948. They were married two years later.

And for a while, she was happy.

While Ralph Tully was dying in the snow banks in Virginia, my father's mother (coincidentally named Virginia) was fleeing her childhood home in Asheville, North Carolina and heading north to Washington, D.C.

Still a teenager when she became pregnant, she was far too immature for the constant demands of motherhood. Her mother, Dolly Nolan Ferguson, became my father's mama, and he grew up in her home in Waynesville, North Carolina, a small town just outside of Asheville.

Eleven years before I was born, the Allied forces of World War II landed in Normandy. My father had just turned eighteen. He'd been in Europe for over a year at that point having been mistakenly drafted at age seventeen due to an error in the family bible recording the year of his birth as 1925, rather than the correct year, 1926. This error changed my father's life. Had his birth year been recorded properly, he would never have been drafted.

My father was the only member of his regiment to survive the war. When the Germans surrendered, he was dispatched to the Black Forest where he helped to free the men, women, and children from the horrors of the Dachau concentration camp.

My father didn't like to talk about the war, and there were only three things I learned of his experience there. The first was about the day his friend was blown up while attempting to deactivate a booby trap on the road. The second was about the first time he found himself eyeball to eyeball with a German soldier. And the third was about the Dachau prisoners, mere walking skeletons, who dropped to the ground and kissed his dusty soldier boots when he entered the concentration camp in the Black Forest.

After the war, my father returned home and attended The University of Virginia on the GI bill. The Dachau experience, together with his university days, led him to believe that education was the single most important gift someone could receive. He passed this belief on through a single sentence I heard him say hundreds, if not thousands, of times.

"They can take everything away from you, but no one can ever take away what's in your brain."

My family situation continued to deteriorate after my birth. By the time I was in kindergarten, it was clear what was happening—my mother was slowly becoming addicted to Valium, having obtained her first prescription after her vertebra shattered when I was born. Our lives descended into a series of excuses, lies and cover-ups. The darkness became so complete that we no longer even noticed the absence of light.

What I discovered as I learned more about the homeless community was that they, too, like me, felt lost in the darkness. The freedom of the wide, now deserted, city streets did not provide any meaningful way to escape these feelings. Wherever they went, however hard they tried to drop out of society, they could not escape themselves.

There was, quite simply, no place to hide.

Not for me. Not for them.

■ – ■ – ■

Maggie Wright, June 2020

When you live on the street, things that you would never have imagined become your reality. This makes you question yourself—who you are and what you stand for. It also shows you exactly how far, and to what lengths, you will go to survive.

William saved my life. He had always been a good friend, but when Rick was arrested and ended up in jail, William stepped up. He did all the things Rick usually did to make sure I was fed and safe, but he did so with a kindness I had not experienced with Rick. It was a stark change.

There was one problem, however. William, the best man I knew, was a thief. There's no two ways about it. That was how he made his money every single day when he was not selling K2 blunts. He was so well-known in the neighborhood that he would literally walk into "his" favorite drug store, and a worker would often raise her hand and say, "Please not today." Whenever William stole the Ensures, it created a lot of paperwork for them.

Stealing is the worst "job" in the world. It is never safe, and there is always the chance that you will be arrested. If William did not come home, I did not have a home. If he was sent to prison, I would be back out on the street. That thought terrified me. I was always scared when he went to "work," my heart pounding, while I waited to see if he got out of the store safely.

To be honest, I hated stealing because of the risk it posed to his safety, and hence to mine. But, I wasn't actually opposed to the act itself. Years on the street had hardened me. Hunger is a motivating factor, and you never know how far you will go to find food until you experience the desperation associated with starvation.

Of course, most people could never understand this, which is why I was so nervous when Traci kept asking what William did to enable us to survive. She knew I was no longer panhandling and was curious. I was surprised at how embarrassed I was to tell her the truth. I had become so used to the act of stealing as part of daily life, I'd forgotten that it is not an acceptable solution for survival.

When I finally told Traci that William was a thief, she was kind, as always. She never judged any of us. She wanted to know more about our lives and how we survived, no matter how horrible and illegal the means were.

But something was changing in me. I started "seeing" myself through Traci's eyes. Her opinion of me became my view of myself. She told me that I was very smart and the fastest reader she knew. I started to think that maybe I should tell her the truth about college—that I'd dropped out in my senior year. Maybe I could go back and finish? Maybe I could have the life that Traci envisioned for me?

PART TWO

I stumbled when I saw.

--GLOUCESTER,
FROM SHAKESPEARE'S *KING LEAR*

CHAPTER 9

Grand Re-Opening

—————■—————

We returned to the city on Monday morning, June 8th, anxious to see what effect the Phase One reopening was having. To our disappointment, as far as we could tell, very little had changed. We thought there would have been, at least, more traffic.

While construction work was allowed to resume, the subject was opaque from the beginning. The rule was that all non-essential construction had to cease unless doing so would present a danger, in which case it was allowed to continue until the point that the danger was eliminated.

We didn't realize that construction had allegedly stopped. During the first three months of the shutdown, we saw it everywhere. Apparently the "gray area" was gray enough to allow construction to, more or less, continue. It would have been hard to argue against the position that abandoning a construction site mid-project in Manhattan might produce a dangerous situation.

Manufacturing and wholesale supply-chain businesses were also allowed to reopen for curbside pickup, in-store pickup or drop-off. Theoretically, one was supposed to have already bought the item that was picked up. However, we saw more than one shopper browsing as they walked through the stores to pay for their item at the cashier's desk, and a fair number of shoppers just "happening" to pick up another item or two as they made their way through the store. No one complained, the least of all, us. We were happy to see some life—any life—returning to our city.

We were grateful that Phase One had begun. Most important, if everything went well in Phase One, Phase Two would begin two weeks later on June 22nd, thus allowing restaurants and hair salons to reopen. I could see that a lot of us were in serious need of haircuts, not to mention dye jobs. I'd never realized that so many New Yorkers colored their hair.

As soon as we parked the car that morning we headed to the apartment to make sandwiches and set out on our morning rounds. The first person we saw was Maggie.

"I messed up again," she said.

"What now?"

"Somehow the bank allowed me to overdraw my balance, and I have a bunch of $34 overdraft charges."

"Geez, I thought a debit card could not be overdrawn?"

"Me, too, which is why I wasn't paying attention," Maggie confessed. I wasn't surprised. Maggie's case worker had explained that homeless people operated on a very short financial in-and-out cycle. When they get money, they spend it because if they don't, it's usually stolen. Saving is not a common practice in the homeless community.

"Let me see your account, please," I asked. Maggie opened up the Chase app on her iPhone and her spending history appeared. There were no large purchases—just a bunch of small ones made here and there.

"Boy, you really didn't buy much of anything," I said.

"Yeah, the most expensive purchase was when I treated myself to some Chinese food."

It would take three more times of reinstating her account and begging Chase to refund the $34 overdraft charges before Maggie would finally learn not to overspend.

Despite the setback with Maggie, Joel agreed to take Mark to Chase to open an account later that morning. A bank account was a pivotal step in reintegrating a homeless person back into society.

"Wow, you look so good," Joel exclaimed when we met up with Mark. To our delight, he was still clean-shaven and wearing a crisp, white golf shirt and a new pair of white sneakers with red accents. More importantly, he had developed a kind of swagger and confidence to his gait. Clean and sober, Mark looked very much like the affluent teenager who'd been raised in Connecticut.

Joel's luck with Mark, however, was not as good as mine had been with Maggie—he wasn't able to open an account for him at Chase, or at any other bank in the area. Each bank required two forms of identification—one with a photo. As easy as that might seem for most Americans, it's virtually an insurmountable task for the homeless. Even Maggie did not have the proper ID. I still wondered how we were able to get her an account with just the letter confirming her identity.

Joel's inability to help Mark solidified my growing awareness of just how hard it is for people to reenter society once they've dropped out. Another eighteen months would pass before we were able to successfully open another bank account for one of our homeless friends.

A few days later, we ran into William and Maggie at 31st Street and Park Avenue. With Rick still in jail, Maggie looked and acted ten years younger despite her recent debit card debacle. William had just moved into his permanent housing in Brooklyn. He liked his two roommates, so we were hopeful that the inevitable fights would be minimal.

"How'd you manage to avoid the quarantine requirement?" Joel asked.

"I was able to get three successive negative COVID tests instead," he replied, triumphantly. I wasn't surprised to learn that William found a way around the rule. He was charismatic and clever. In fact, he'd been able to get his permanent housing in part by claiming he was depressed. Homeless people who are certified with a mental illness, like women in danger of domestic violence, were given higher priority in housing assignments.

A few months before we'd met him, William had checked himself into a mental institution and convinced the doctors that he might hurt himself. While William did have a significant drinking problem, he did not appear to be depressed. Au contraire, as far as we could tell William always had a smile on his face.

Maggie showed us pictures of his new place. The apartment had three bedrooms, one bathroom, a living room, and a kitchen. From the pictures she showed us, it appeared to be in an old building with wooden floors and high ceilings. A single mattress, still in its wrapping, was in William's room along with a small, used dresser. Maggie said the kitchen was stocked with the basics—pots and pans, utensils, dishes, cutlery, and glasses.

Best of all, Maggie was allowed to sleep there. Whereas only the person assigned to a safe haven room is allowed entry, permanent housing becomes a person's home, and guests are welcome. Maggie was bubbling with excitement.

"We made tacos last night and watched *Joker*," she said with pride.

"How did you do that?"

"I downloaded it on the iPhone, then streamed it to the TV."

"Wow, aren't you resourceful!" I exclaimed with a certain parental pride. Despite our friendship, I was almost thirty years older than Maggie. It had been less than three months since I found her sweeping the sidewalk, and I was proud of how far she'd come in such a short period of time.

"Not to spoil the mood here, but I have bad news, Tray. Rick is getting out of jail tomorrow," Maggie said, with a frown similar to that of a person who's just bitten into a lemon wedge.

"Who put up the bail money?"

"Some lawyers' group."

"Good for Rick, but please stay away from him," I urged. William nodded in agreement.

Later that morning, we were scheduled to talk with Kyle's case worker, Karen, in Madison Square Park. We had agreed on meeting at the Fifth Avenue corner. When we arrived, we were unsure whether Karen meant the corner of the street or the corner of the park, so I sat down on a bench at the park corner, and Joel stood on the street. Exactly at the appointed hour of our meeting, I saw a woman approaching, smiling warmly.

"Miss Traci!" she shouted.

I wondered how she knew who I was. She must have sensed my confusion because she laughed and said, "I Googled you and found your picture."

I waved at Joel and motioned for him to come over. The three of us sat on a park bench for an hour reviewing our journal. Karen took careful notes, promising to assign case workers to Tony, Cathy and Bob, the three remaining members of our little group who did not yet have one.

"What about Ed and Tammy?" Joel asked. "Can they get case workers too?"

"They're already registered with another agency," Karen said. "And they have a case worker."

"Why are they still on the street then?" I asked.

"I'm sorry to have to tell you this. They did have a room but were recently evicted due to a DV charge against Ed."

"What's a DV?" I asked.

"A domestic violence charge."

"Does this permanently disqualify them from future housing?" Joel asked.

"That depends on the severity of the charge," Karen said. "I'm going to call their case worker next week and see what I can find out."

Just as we were about to leave, Karen said, "Wait, did you just say you know Henry?"

"Yes," I said.

"We have a room for him! The transportation team is coming tomorrow morning at ten a.m. to pick him up. Do you think you can find him and give him the message? Ask him to be waiting on the east side of Park and 28th Street."

I couldn't believe it! Henry had been homeless for eight years, and tomorrow, he would be getting a room. He'd recently told us that his current situation had nothing to do with getting a bad start in life. Rather, he'd had a happy childhood, growing up in a loving home with two older sisters and one younger brother. His mother was a hairdresser, and his father, a transit worker. Henry followed his mother's profession and became a barber. He managed three separate locations before opening up a shop of his own.

After his marriage to Ellen ended, Henry started boxing professionally in the featherweight class. His face showed every scar. He was nevertheless a handsome sixty-two-year-old man. The emotional and physical blows he'd endured, along with his failed marriage and injured knee, eventually led him to heroin and stealing to pay for it. He was caught and sentenced to twenty-five years in prison for armed robbery. In 2011, he was released after serving twenty years.

Upon his release, Henry bounced from shelter to shelter for the next year. Finally, the stress of the shelter system—the fights, the noise, the robberies—drove him to the streets, which, like Maggie and Rick, he considered safer. For the most part, Henry avoided heroin but began using crack when he could afford it, as well as K2. He panhandled endlessly to pay for the drugs, often yelling at pedestrians who refused to give him money.

"What do you mean you won't give me money for something to eat? Can't you see that I'm starving?"

Despite his twenty years in prison and his drug addictions, Henry appeared to be in good physical shape. So when he'd gotten really sick in February, Maggie had been quick to intervene.

"I made him go to the hospital because I thought he was having a heart attack from smoking too much crack. He'd been having difficulty breathing, but the virus was still new, and we didn't really know much about it back then. Turned out, he had COVID. He was the first one of us to get it."

"And he listened to you?"

"You better believe he listened. I saved him many years ago when he'd almost overdosed on heroin."

"Are you kidding me? I thought he wasn't using heroin?"

"It was just that once, as far as I know. It happened one night when eight of us chipped in for a hotel room in the middle of a snow storm. We got a suite with two beds in each room. Next thing I knew, Henry had a needle in his arm, and before I could get to him, he'd shot up. I knew something was wrong before the needle dropped from his hand."

"How'd you know so quickly?"

"He turned blue and stopped breathing."

"Oh, I guess that is a clue. How did you save him?"

"I had Narcan and gave it to him, but he didn't respond. Then one of the guys filled a syringe with water and salt and injected into his temple. This brought him around a bit, although he was still out of it."

"I can't believe you could inject salt into someone's temple and have anything good come out of it," I said.

"Well, that is what we did," Maggie replied, shrugging her shoulders.

"What did you do next?"

"We offered him some crack. He took one hit and sat straight up like nothing had happened."

"Did he say anything?"

"Yeah, he asked us why we all looked so scared. And then he asked for another hit of crack."

"You couldn't make this stuff up," I said and laughed so hard the tears ran down my face. Then I caught myself. There was nothing funny about Maggie's story. And I wasn't at all sure it was even medically possible.

That morning, however, despite his incarcerations, drug use and plain old bad luck, Henry had hit the homeless lottery, and Karen was anxious to find him.

"We'll find him," Joel promised.

"Thanks so much! And by the way, I'm also looking for Tony. Do you know where to find him?"

Just as we were explaining Tony's work schedule and when he could be found in the bodega on Second Avenue, he appeared out of nowhere across the street. I jumped up from the bench, ran across the street forgetting to look for traffic, and intercepted Tony who, per usual, was intent on getting to work on time. He was skinny as a teenage track star, which was no surprise because he ran everywhere. That morning was no exception, and Tony was not interested in being detained.

"Can you talk for a few minutes with a case worker?" I asked.

Tony was nervous but followed me. He'd been homeless for twenty-four years and had suffered his share of shattered hopes and dreams while living on the street. He was only fifty-two but appeared older despite his ability to run well. Missing teeth, a tapestry of scars and imbedded dirt marred his otherwise handsome face.

Tony was born in Puerto Rico and moved to Newark, New Jersey with his parents, brother and sister when he was a baby. He never graduated from high school, instead dropping out to work odd construction jobs when he was sixteen. He started drinking after work to dull the soreness in his body from hauling heavy materials all day. Two years later, he became a heroin addict. The addiction led to Tony's continuous tardiness and absences from work, as well as an estrangement from his family. By the time he was twenty-two, Tony had lost his job and was suddenly homeless.

To try to turn his life around, Tony came to New York to live with his brother and his brother's wife. His brother was an alcoholic, and when the two of them were drunk, rip-roaring fights were the inevitable outcome. One day, his brother threw him out at the insistence of his wife who had threatened to withhold marital privileges until Tony was gone.

Tony left the next morning, and it wasn't long before he started selling drugs. He ended up in prison and served seven years. When he got out in 2008, he kept to himself and tried to stay out of trouble. He started collecting cans for money and working at various bodegas in exchange for food. He used the money he got from collecting cans to pay the rent for his small storage unit. On really cold nights, he'd slip into the unit if no one was looking. The storage owner never bothered him, and the police never knocked on his door.

When we met him, Tony had been clean for twelve years with the help of methadone, a legal synthetic opioid, which he received from Greenwich House, a rehab clinic on Mercer Street in the heart of Greenwich Village. Despite his addictions, incarcerations, and nerves, Tony made a good first impression that morning, and Karen was anxious to help him get his first safe haven room.

Karen motioned for us to sit down, and we positioned Tony in between us. He was visibly shaking. Joel reached over my lap and patted him on the knee. Karen was gracious and kind and told Tony that he would be assigned a case worker very soon. She then went on to explain how the safe haven rooms were assigned and promised to find one for him.

Tony was nodding, but I could tell by the way he was staring off into the distance that he wasn't really paying attention to Karen. He probably didn't believe her. Who would be surprised? Tony had been living on the streets of New York City for twenty-four years and had never even been able to get a case worker, much less a safe haven room.

Ten minutes later, our conversation over, Tony went skipping off to work. Karen shook her head and said, "You two are homeless magnets."

"Well, it's amazing who shows up when we do," I replied.

"That's actually the secret," she said. "No matter what they do or don't do, you just have to keep showing up for them." Those words burned brightly inside my mind. And into my heart. I would recall them hundreds of times in the following months.

We said our goodbyes a second time and headed back up Park Avenue, stopping to check on Bob and Cathy. Suddenly, Maggie appeared, and I asked her to find Henry and give him the good news that he was getting a safe haven room the following day. At this point, Maggie, anxious to help others, had become a valuable asset to us as she knew everyone, what they were up to, and where they were. And whenever I asked her to check on someone, she saluted and completed the task quickly.

"I'll find him," she promised and skittered off.

Later that evening, Maggie called as we were about to sit down for dinner.

"I found him," she shouted so loudly that Joel heard her voice booming through my cell phone across the room. "He'll be waiting on the street corner tomorrow morning."

"Oh, that is so exciting!" I exclaimed. "Joel and I are going to be there, too, to send him off."

"William and I will be there also," she promised.

Joel and I went to bed happy that night. William and Maggie were sheltered. Henry would be by noon the following day. Mark had a job, a room, and a great case worker. Kyle had Karen in his corner, and she was working to place him in a safe haven room. Karen had promised to have case workers assigned to Bob, Cathy, and Tony. She also said she would look into the domestic violence violation against Ed and Tammy.

But Rick was getting out of jail the next morning. And I was sure this was not going to turn out well.

On Thursday, we started our morning with an unexpected phone call from Henry.

"For eight years I've been homeless. No matter what I did, nothing happened. I just can't believe I'm getting a room today!"

"We're so happy for you, Henry. We'll be down in ten minutes to see you off," Joel promised.

"You two made this happen," Henry muttered in between sobs.

"You did it, Henry. We just helped."

When we reached the corner, we saw Henry pacing nervously, his emotions clearly bouncing between glee and terror. William and Maggie showed up five minutes later. Unfortunately, Rick, as I'd feared, was also there. We offered him a sandwich.

"Am I entitled?" he asked, hesitating as he accepted my offering. I was unsure whether Rick was just nervous about being back on the street, or embarrassed that we knew he'd spent a month in jail for assault and battery.

"Sure, here you go," I said. I felt bad for Rick, despite his transgressions. I knew he had a rough life and that beneath his temper, he had a warm heart. We're all victims of victims, I reminded myself more than once.

Rick had barely eaten his sandwich when we saw him offer Henry some K2.

"Henry, can't you wait until after they take you to your room?" Maggie shouted.

"I only took one hit," Henry said, defending himself.

"No hits this morning, Henry. No hits," Maggie yelled and then proceeded to flirt with Rick.

William walked away, clearly pissed. I was angry too. Despite Maggie's flirtatious behavior, Rick was in a foul mood and picked a fight with a young man named Vincent who was standing next to Henry. The situation became more and more agitated and suddenly, Rick ripped the sandwich bag we'd given Vincent out of his hand and flung it over his own shoulder, hitting my right eye. I was glad we'd used fresh, soft bread to make the sandwiches that morning. It startled me but did not cause any damage.

Vincent ran into the middle of 28th Street and was almost hit by a truck. Shaken, he knocked the truck driver's side mirror off, flipped him the bird, and dropped several F-bombs in the process. The negative energy continued to cycle. The driver stopped the truck, jumped out, and ran after Vincent. Joel ran after the truck driver, intercepting him a half block up Park Avenue.

I turned to Maggie and she knew I was not happy. "Rick messes up everything he touches. Stay away from him."

Joel managed to calm the truck driver, and we turned our attention back to what was supposed to be the joyous event of the morning. Henry was being housed in the Andrews, a homeless shelter located downtown at 197 Bowery. A former lodging house built in 1901, the Andrews was now being used as transitional housing for the homeless. It had 146 short-term housing units. In addition to housing, clients also received on-site counseling, three meals a day, and access to free laundry services.

A few minutes after the appointed hour, the transportation car pulled up. We all hugged Henry and told him we'd see him later that day once he was situated. He hopped into the back seat of the car like a five-year-old going to Kindergarten. I motioned for him to roll down the window so I could take his picture. The back seat was covered in plastic, and there was a protective barrier separating Henry from the two employees who sat in the front. Henry was clearly very nervous, and we all gave him the "thumbs-up" sign as the light turned green and the car drove away.

Later that day, Maggie reported that Henry had arrived at the Andrews safely, loved his room, and was doing well. At the time, I thought everything was set. I did not realize how tenuous that first step was. A person was required to use the room—or at least to sign in at the front desk—once every three days or risk losing it. As easy as such a requirement might seem, it proved more difficult than I could have imagined, especially in the summer months when the weather was pleasant and the incentive to avoid the cold was gone. And, after years of sleeping on the street, the homeless grew accustomed to it.

That night Joel and I did some more research about the causes of homelessness. We made a list of the people we knew and the circumstances leading to their living on the streets. Each person's story was different, but we were able to group them into four general categories—substance abuse, sudden loss of employment leading to an inability to pay rent, breakdown in a domestic situation and mental illness.

Our categories were almost identical to the list. The national causes listed a fifth—physical disability—which we hadn't encountered, except for Bob's swollen legs and feet. We thought of the friends we'd made and their backgrounds. Henry, Tony, and Maggie had become homeless as a result of addiction; Bob due to sudden unemployment; Cathy experienced a breakdown in her domestic situation when her mother died. Kyle had run away from home when his parents' abuse escalated to a point that he feared for his life. Rick, like Bob, had lost his job during the financial crisis in 2008.

The following morning Rick was back panhandling on his old corner, despite an injunction that prohibited him from doing so. His court date was scheduled for June 18th. I doubted he would show up.

Maggie and William were waiting for us across the street. As we approached them, Rick crossed Park Avenue carrying a book in his outstretched hand—a peace offering for Maggie. I saw the title, *The Secret*. I knew Maggie would like that book, and she gladly accepted Rick's gift.

William was not happy; neither were we. In the past three years, Rick had only managed to give Maggie broken bones, black eyes, and a brain injury that had led to her continuing loss of taste and smell. Suddenly, he emerged from jail bearing gifts?

Despite Rick's release from jail, there was more reason to celebrate on Tuesday, June 16th when we learned that Bob had been assigned a case worker, Alvin, who had already found a safe haven room for him at the Andrews!

The next morning, Bob was back in his phone booth, sitting upright and looking proud. He was feeling so good about himself that he was going to visit his mother that afternoon and had even managed to scrape together enough money to buy her a small gift at the dollar store—a serving plate.

"My mom will like this," he said with pride, holding up the plate. "She's a real good cook."

Bob ended up spending two nights with his mother. When we saw him on Friday morning, we reminded him that he had to check in to his room by 2 p.m. that day. I didn't want to bug him the first thing in the morning but couldn't stop myself.

"Did you check in to your room yesterday?" I asked.

"Nah, I don't like the place that much," Bob mumbled.

"What's wrong with it? Henry is there, and he likes it."

"Everyone is smoking K2 in the bathrooms. And my stuff isn't safe."

Bob drank his fair share of vodka, but he did not use drugs and really didn't like to be around people who did.

"You've only slept there one night," Joel said. "You need to give it more time before you decide you can't be there."

I tried to get Bob to agree to call his case worker and promise he would be checking into his room that night. "You need to sign in today or you're going to lose the room, Bob. You might not care now, but you sure will once winter comes around again. And besides, all you have to do is show up once every three days and check in. You can go up to your room and immediately leave if you want."

Bob nodded as if he agreed. Nevertheless, he never made it to his room and lost it the following week. Undeterred, Joel and I spoke to Alvin, who amazingly, found another room for Bob in the Bronx the following week. But Bob turned it down citing the poor living conditions in the neighborhood.

"I'm not living in that rat-infested drug zone."

We were heart-broken. Bob was so close to getting off the streets. And suddenly, he was back at the end of the line. We doubted that he'd be offered a third room. With so many people in need, there were only so many chances a person could reasonably expect.

Nevertheless, the agency arranged for a nurse to visit Bob on the street corner every week. Nurse Betty brought his medicines and made sure he understood when to take them. Within a few weeks, a significant amount of the fluid in Bob's legs had drained, and he regained a fair amount of his mobility.

Concerns over Chad's upcoming surgery—the removal of his gall-bladder—had diverted our attention away from Bob's health issues for a few days. The operation was scheduled for the morning of June 18th. Even though this would be his seventh surgery since the accident, Joel and I were nervous when we woke up.

As a distraction, we decided to make our rounds again until we received the phone call from his doctor. It was a long day of waiting for that call. We spent it canvassing, looking for other homeless people that were not yet part of the shelter system. We carried the Verification of Homelessness forms with us, filled them out with men and women on the street, and emailed screenshots to Karen, Kyle's case worker. Both Karen and Maggie's case worker, Lina, were excellent at their jobs and helped us with our efforts to assist, not only their clients, but also the others in our group, as well.

I was also secretly on the lookout for Rick that morning. He was due to show up for his court hearing at ten a.m. I might have called the police if I'd run into him, but despite the hours we spent walking the streets, I did not see him.

Just before dinner, Chad's surgeon finally called with the good news that Chad was fine and could come home if he was feeling up to it. Later that evening, Joel picked him up from the hospital entrance. When he ambled in through the front door, I breathed a sigh of relief. Two years and seven surgeries later, Chad had become a matrix of scars that crossed his torso. None of that mattered that night. Chad was alive and this was something we no longer took as a given.

The following morning, Chad woke up feeling okay, and Governor Cuomo gave his final daily briefing. It was his 111th. "Today, we have done a full 180, from worst to first. We are controlling the virus better than any state in the country and any nation on the globe."

More welcome news followed later that day when Kyle's case worker, Karen, called and told us she hoped to have a room for him the following week. I wondered if maybe she was trying to secure Bob's old room at the Andrews before someone else grabbed it. Competition for the safe haven rooms was always tight.

The up-and-down seesaw that had come to define our lives tipped in the wrong direction later that day when Maggie disappeared. I called, texted and sent emails, all to no avail. I knew that meant trouble. The next day, she confessed that she'd drank too much and had spent the day detoxing.

On June 21st, the sun was still high in the sky at eight p.m. I went outside and watched the glowing, orange ball slowly drop into the Hudson River, basking the east-west city streets in its diminishing essence.

The Phase Two reopening was on schedule to begin the following day, and city residents looked forward to dining in a restaurant again. Many people, including us, hoped the worst was behind us.

For some New Yorkers, that proved true.

Unfortunately, for others, the worst was still to come.

■ – ■ – ■

Maggie Wright, June 2020

I always had a soft spot for Henry, which is why it was so important for me to be there on his big day. He'd been on the streets for a long time. I'd literally watched him almost die from an overdose one night. It was the first, and only, time I dropped to my knees and prayed to a higher power. So there was no way I was going to miss his big day, even though I knew I was looking for trouble.

Rick had been released from jail, and I knew he'd be at his usual spot looking for me. Coincidentally, the usual spot was only one block north of where the transport van was coming to pick up Henry. That was the first piece of bad luck that day.

It had been a month since Rick was arrested. Rick had been hiding from the police all day. He'd assaulted a pedestrian with that pipe of his, and a warrant was out for his arrest.

That evening, the police finally found him. When they cuffed him and took him away in the police car, my entire body started shaking, uncontrollably. I was living on the streets on my own. I had to make all the money, and there was no one to ensure that I was safe. Ironically, Rick posed the greatest danger to my safety for the last three years. Sadly, however, I loved Rick and had since I was a young girl.

Rick is ten years older than me, and as a young girl, he was my hero. Our fathers are first cousins so I guess that makes us second cousins. But we saw each other all the time at family functions. We shared a history, a family, and a love of science. We'd shared a life on the streets for three years. When he wasn't beating me up, I enjoyed our conversations and his company.

However, things with William were going really well. I was officially living with him in Brooklyn, and for the first time in years, I felt safe and happy. When he got word that he had been given housing, he took me with him the first time he saw the place. He wanted to make sure it was never "his home" but "ours." I was so grateful to have a roof over my head I didn't even know what to do with myself the first night I'd slept there. I loved the apartment, and I stayed in bed all night, staring at the ceiling, marveling that there was one over my head.

As we left our apartment that morning, I confessed to William that I was nervous we might run into Rick. William was not happy. I assured him I was done with Rick, but to be honest, I wasn't so sure. I wanted to be done with Rick, but it wasn't that easy. I felt he deserved another chance—one last chance. I was torn and conflicted as to where my loyalty should lie.

As the subway approached Midtown, my anxiety grew. I knew Traci and Joel would be there, and if they saw Rick, things would not go smoothly. Rick had already assaulted them with his pipe once before, and I did not trust him to not repeat the behavior.

As William and I made our way to the corner, I saw Henry, Traci and Joel waiting. Henry was pacing around in circles. And naturally, Rick was there too. When I saw him, my heart jumped. His month in jail had detoxed him. He looked clean, sober and healthy. He'd even gained some weight, which was no surprise. One "advantage" of jail is that you get fed.

As soon as he saw me, he came over and was putting on his best charm. I could not deny I was happy to see him. The next thing I knew, I was flirting with him. Traci scowled and William walked away shaking his head. But I couldn't stop. I kept up my flirtation.

But then Rick realized that William and I were "together" and became enraged. As I watched his face contort in anger, I knew we were done. Any infatuation, love or feelings for Rick were gone in an instant. I was not dealing with his rage ever again.

Just like Henry, that day was a new beginning for me. Henry was going to his new home. I was already in mine.

CHAPTER 10

Fading Sun

───────■───────

Restaurants were very negatively affected during the pandemic—over half did not survive the first shutdown. New York City eateries were scheduled to reopen on June 22nd, the first day of Phase Two. When the much-awaited date arrived, however, Mayor de Blasio announced that only outdoor dining would be allowed. Nevertheless, restaurant owners went to work and, seemingly overnight, the city sidewalks were transformed into beautiful outdoor dining venues.

The energy of the city underwent a metamorphosis in the process. The sidewalk cafes made the streets feel more reminiscent of Paris than ones in the middle of a pandemic. While some people complained about the inability to dine inside, few people found it objectionable to enjoy a meal al fresco. The timing was as perfect as the weather that June. Dry, hot days cooled off at night and the outdoor dining venues, twinkling with lights, provided a bustling, lively atmosphere throughout the city. A crack appeared in an otherwise shuttered and depressed environment. Light filtered into the city, and with it, a hope that was palpable.

My law partner, Peter, and I decided to eat lunch outside every day, rather than at our desks, in order to support the struggling business owners and their employees in our area. The social distancing requirement ensured that tables were well-spaced, thus preventing other diners from overhearing our conversations. On the rare occasion when we needed to discuss a particularly sensitive issue, we passed written messages back and forth across the table, reminding us of our corporate days when exchanging yellow sticky notes during long meetings was a matter of routine. And in any event, that was rarely necessary. We left generous tips wherever we went, our small way of helping the thousands of servers and other restaurant workers get back on their feet.

Despite the abundance of outdoor dining venues, it was apparent that restaurants were struggling. Very few corporate businesses had reopened, and even fewer New York City residents were in town. On many of our outings, we were the only two people in the restaurant. There were, however, many masked and glove-wearing servers anxiously awaiting customers.

I began to doubt whether the restaurant Joel and I had opened in Mahopac ten years earlier would make it. So when my good friend, and previous restaurant partner Jan had called the month before with the news I'd been expecting, I had not been surprised. The restaurant was closing. Even though we'd already sold our share of the business to our partners, Jan and her husband, Ramiro, remained our close friends. I was heartbroken for them and knew that the loss of the restaurant income would have negative consequences on their budget.

■ – ■ – ■

June 2010. When I'd first declared we really were moving ahead with the plans we'd been discussing for the last ten years, Joel was skeptical.

"What do you know about the restaurant business, Ms. Patent Litigator?"

I had to admit the truth—not a single thing. Nevertheless, my desire to make another name for myself in the professional world following my retirement fanned the fire of my obstinacy. I had the perfect plan. Or so I thought.

Jan had been our children's nanny so I knew her work ethic well—she was undoubtedly one of the hardest working women I'd ever known. Ramiro was a well-respected chef.

Our dream culminated in the opening of Ramiro's 954 (our chef's name coupled with the street address) on February 8, 2011. Not surprisingly, our reality entailed a lot more work and a lot less satisfaction than the dream we'd nourished, even if the restaurant had earned a "Don't Miss" review from one of the incognito *New York Times* reviewers.

Joel and I drove up from the city on the weekends. Most of the time we'd sit in the bar in case an extra pair of hands was needed. On busy nights, I'd dust off my waitress shoes and pick up an order pad to help out. It was a humbling experience waiting tables after a thirty-year legal career. I even found myself on all fours on the bathroom floor cleaning up paper towels and toilet paper that had missed the bowl. Whatever it takes, I'd remind myself when the stench became overwhelming.

The legal profession isn't exactly easy. In our restaurant, however, the concept of working hard took on a whole new meaning. Most nights I could barely drag myself home when the doors closed. One night, the restaurant was filling up fast. Jan came bustling over.

"Hey, Traci, can you take the bar section tables tonight, please?" It was not a question. She needed me on the floor as soon as I could change my shoes.

I slid off my stool and grabbed a pad. I couldn't remember orders without writing them down, unlike the more seasoned servers. That surprised me as I could remember every single fact about complicated lawsuits. I already had a customer by the time I was ready to take the first order.

He was a regular, a man who always dined alone while reading a book. He rarely looked up except when ordering or paying his bill. I knew what he drank—cranberry juice and seltzer, with a lime. I placed the beverage down in front of his lowered head.

"I hope you don't mind," I said somewhat hesitantly while making a wide arc with my right arm over the vibrating restaurant, "we're swamped and your regular server is upstairs so I'm taking this section tonight."

"No problem, darling," he said in his British accent. Flooded with relief, I attempted to make a joke.

"Here's something else to read." I handed him a menu. He took it and chuckled.

"I think I know this one by heart." It was my turn to laugh.

"Well, I guess you're a good reader," I quipped. "My partner told me that you're also a writer."

"I'm actually more of an editor." He held out his hand. "Richard Kelley."

I smiled and shook his outstretched offering.

"I'm Traci. I've seen you in the restaurant before; it's nice to finally meet you. I'm actually trying to write my first book and getting nowhere fast," I confessed.

"Richard Kelley, the editor, at your service," he said, handing me his business card.

A few hours later, I arrived home, kicking off my sticky-soled waitress shoes as I shut the front door behind me. Too tired to shower, I fell into bed in my shirt, reeking of sweat and cooking grease.

What have I gotten myself into this time?

Sleep arrived before I could brush my teeth.

Despite ten years of success, the restaurant was now closing and, as I feared, the effect on Jan and Ramiro was immediate. With the restaurant income suddenly eliminated from their budget, they were unable to pay their bills. Jan's health started to decline. She was only fifty-five, but she seemed to have aged ten years in less than a month.

"I can't go on much longer," she confided to me one night. "The financial stress is literally killing me."

"Can't you get one of those COVID-relief loans from the government?" I asked.

"I've tried. Nothing."

"What about unemployment?"

"I can't get that either because I'm the owner."

"Maybe you should consider filing for bankruptcy?" I suggested.

Jan agreed and consulted with a bankruptcy attorney the next morning. Two days later, she was hospitalized with acute stomach pain that left her unable to eat.

The following week my editor, Richard, called to say that he, too, was under extreme financial stress and had been hospitalized with a strange lump in his shoulder. I wondered how many more of my friends would be affected by the financial stress of the shutdown, not to mention the virus itself, before the pandemic was over.

The warmth of the summer solstice did not last long, literally or figuratively. First, Henry disappeared. He hadn't checked into his safe haven room in a week and no one knew where he was.

"He's going to lose his room, if he hasn't already," I said.

"I know, but what can we do? Everyone is looking for him," Joel replied.

"It's just so frustrating. Eight years of living on the streets and he finally has a room and then disappears. Maggie said she has looked all over the city for him."

"Bob, Cathy, and Tony are looking for him too," Joel said. "He often comes by their telephone booth to hang out when he's not panhandling."

Maggie was the next person to disappear. When I hadn't heard from her in three days, I started to worry. *Where was she? Was she alright?* When she finally called, she reported that she had a black eye, bruised ribs, and a smashed cell phone from another encounter with Rick.

"I'm sorry, Tray, I messed up again."

"Just keep trying to try," I encouraged her. "Most of the so-called progress I've made in this life has been on my hands and knees, crawling towards the light, begging for mercy."

"How can you still love me after everything I've done?" Maggie asked.

"This probably sounds corny, but everything good has love at the center of it. It's the key to healing. To forgiveness. Even to courage."

"You're absolutely right," Maggie agreed. "I just don't feel worthy of it."

We agreed to meet the next morning at our usual spot on Park Avenue. As Joel and I approached, we saw Maggie and a young man in what appeared to be a heated argument. I could hear her voice from a block away. William was standing with his back against the wall of a building, watching the spectacle unfold.

"I'm not talking to you with a needle in your arm," Maggie yelled, pointing her finger in the man's face. The young man looked confused, smiled sheepishly, and started to back away. "Really, Mike, I'm serious. Have some respect for pedestrians and go around the corner to shoot up."

Hearing Maggie's admonition was a watershed moment for me. Despite her good judgment in telling Mike he shouldn't shoot up in the middle of Park Avenue, I was disappointed with her for going anywhere near Rick. It was clear that Maggie could discern the right thing to do, yet, like many of us, she could not always put her good judgment to the best use when it came to her own actions. As I got closer, I saw her black eye.

"When are you going to learn that you need to stay away from Rick?" I asked with a harsher tone than I'd intended.

"I know, I know. I'm done with him. I promise." William shook his head and snorted in disgust. "I tried to tell her," he said.

Rick's hearing had been postponed. The courts were still essentially closed and the few proceedings that were taking place were being conducted on Zoom.

There was a positive development that week, however. Phase Two had produced a noticeable shift in the energy of the city. In addition to the outdoor dining, barber shops and hair salons reopened. Lines snaked out of the barber shops and around the nearest corner. Likewise, the hair salons were busy. Unfortunately, the lines only lasted a week. The pent-up demand for haircuts and dye jobs was quickly satisfied and barbers and hair stylists soon found their chairs empty once again.

Places of worship were also allowed to reopen (at twenty-five percent capacity), as were businesses in the finance and insurance industries. Likewise, real estate offices opened their doors, even though there were very few people looking to rent or buy apartments in the city at the time. The mass exodus was still in full force. It was hard to blame anyone. New York City had become a war zone.

Notably absent from the Phase Two list were nail salons, which were scheduled to reopen in Phase Three, along with indoor dining. Once again, I was aware that the most vulnerable workers were often the most negatively affected by the shutdown. Most women working in nail salons appeared to be Hispanic or Asian. Likewise, most restaurant employees were young, many aspiring actors or undocumented immigrants. I wondered how many of them would qualify for unemployment. How could they withstand a virtual lack of income for months?

Broadway announced that its closure would last through the end of the year. Thousands of actors and other theater employees were without any hope of employment, at least in the theater business, for the foreseeable future. It would turn out to be another fifteen months before the first show on Broadway would reopen.

Movie theaters and museums also remained shuttered, and large entertainment venues such as Madison Square Garden and Carnegie Hall were indefinitely closed.

Joel and I continued our efforts to help our homeless friends obtain shelter. At the end of June, Kyle's case worker, Karen, called on a Friday afternoon with the news we'd been hoping to hear.

"We finally have a room for Kyle!" she exclaimed in obvious delight. I knew she'd been working for months to place him in a safe haven room. "I need your help, please. I couldn't find him when I went out earlier today. Do you think you can tell him the transportation van will be by at five o'clock to pick him up.?"

"We're not in the city, but our son, Chad, is, and he's friends with Kyle. I will ask him to track him down," I offered.

"Great, thanks so much!"

Chad scoured the neighborhood for the next several hours. It was dinnertime, and we were about to tell him to call it a day when my phoned dinged. A text message from Karen arrived—*Chad found him! Kyle is sheltered!*" We opened a bottle of our best red wine to celebrate.

Kyle had been homeless for fifteen years. I slept soundly that night knowing he was in a bed with sheets and a pillow. It was clear to me that my feelings for Kyle had definitely evolved into a mother's concern for a child. At the same moment I wondered again what type of alternate reality I had entered, and whether it was going to be possible for me to ever go back to my life, pre-COVID.

On Monday morning, Kyle was back in his spot panhandling, looking clean and rested.

"How did it feel to sleep in a bed?" Joel asked.

"It felt wonderful."

When we returned to the apartment that afternoon after making our rounds, Joel called Mark and asked him to stop by after dinner. At this point, several of our homeless friends knew we lived in Murray Hill, and while we never met anyone near our building, we would meet on the corner at Park Avenue.

Over the weekend, we'd gathered together bags of Joel's barely-worn clothes, old sheets and towels, extra pots and pans, and other basic supplies for Mark's apartment. We splurged on an air conditioning unit for his window.

After Mark arrived, we called an Uber, loaded the items into it, and sent him on his way to Harlem, surrounded by his new possessions. As the car pulled away, he stuck his arm out of the window, made a fist and pumped it up and down in the air. The joy of watching him ride off hung in the summer air long after we said goodbye.

A few days later, however, the "Mark joy" evaporated when he called Joel. "Bad news. My apartment has bed bugs and the landlord said I have to vacate by the end of the week."

As his eviction day approached, Mark became agitated, afraid he would end up homeless again. Both he and Joel searched the ads, looking for another room to rent in his neighborhood but found nothing Mark could afford.

At the last minute, his case worker came through and found a room for him at The Travelers, the same location where Maggie was sheltered. Most of his clothes, sheets and towels could not go with him, however, due to the bed bugs. Likewise, AC units were not allowed, so he returned it to us.

At least his new room was free. He'd be saving almost $700 a month in rent expense. In addition, he'd be getting three free meals a day and laundry service on Thursdays. Best of all, The Travelers was walking distance from our apartment building, and Joel was busy talking with the superintendents on our street looking for extra work for Mark.

The following week, Joel found Mark a job as a custodian in one of the large apartment buildings. He worked there two days each week. The other five days, he continued to work in the Bronx. With no rent and seven days of paid work, he was in the best shape he'd been in since losing his wife.

While we celebrated Mark's good luck, and the extra cash in his pocket, a persistent villain was lurking to take it all away.

New Yorkers anxiously awaited the Phase Three reopening scheduled for July 6th. The number of new cases in the city remained low, with single-digit daily deaths becoming the norm rather than the exception. Nevertheless, the virus was surging in places like Florida, Texas and Arizona, and it was increasingly apparent that New Yorkers would be affected.

Nine states considered hot spots were put on a "bad boy" list. Anyone entering New York from those areas was required to self-quarantine for fourteen days. The penalty for non-compliance was a heavy fine; how that was to be enforced was unclear.

Two days later, Mayor de Blasio confirmed what we feared—the return of indoor dining was delayed, and not only by a week, as Governor Cuomo had alluded to two days earlier, but indefinitely. The mayor attempted to justify his last-minute decision by saying that the science indicated the virus spread more easily indoors.

In an effort to quell the growing resentment, de Blasio promised to "double-down" on outdoor dining spaces, allowing restaurants to set up tables not only on sidewalks but in the curb lane of the streets, as well. While there might have been more restaurant seats available, this did little to placate some New Yorkers who were eager to enjoy a meal out of the ninety degree heat. Restaurant owners, who were already struggling to cover their rents, were also angry.

Of more immediate concern to us was Jan's declining health. She had been in and out of the hospital several times by this point, and her undiagnosed stomach ailment was not improving. Equally upsetting was the fact that Bob reported Cathy was hospitalized with an acute case of bronchitis.

A few days later, Bob's spirits lifted when Cathy called from the hospital with the news that she was being released later that day. Unfortunately, his relief, as well as ours, did not last long—Cathy did not return to the telephone booth, as we all expected. Bob was despondent and became increasingly agitated as the days went by without word from her.

"Don't worry, Bob, Joel said in an effort to assuage his fears. "Cathy has disappeared before. She'll be back."

"I messed up my marriage and wouldn't even know my own daughter if she walked by," he said with tears in his eyes that kept flowing despite his obvious attempts to stem them. Suddenly, it made sense why Bob was so attentive to Cathy. She was the daughter he never knew, and he was going to make sure he did not mess up a second time.

I decided to broach a subject I'd been avoiding for months. "Bob, why don't you know where your daughter is?"

Bob looked down and the tears started up again. He sniffled and coughed. Nevertheless, I stood on the street in front of him waiting for his answer.

"I went to prison for fifteen years when she was only six," he said. "When I got out, she and her mother had moved away. I don't even know where they are."

"Fifteen years," I sputtered before I could stop myself. "What did you do?"

"Me and some of my friends robbed a liquor store. My friend shot the owner. Thankfully, he didn't die."

I tried to appear nonchalant, though my head was spinning. *What are you doing out here, woman? Most of these people are felons, drug addicts, or both.* In an effort to keep the conversation rooted in compassion, I changed the subject.

"When you got out of prison, were you homeless?"

"Yes. I used to sleep in that marble church on Fifth Avenue. Then I got me that job in the hardware store and things were okay for a while until my boss died nine years ago."

"And you've been homeless ever since, right?"

"Yeah. I'm real sorry I'm homeless. I wanted more for my life. I worked hard in college and played real good football. I feel real sorry, especially for putting my mother through this. If you don't own your own land though, you're homeless."

"Well, don't worry," Joel promised. "Traci and I are not giving up until we get you sheltered. We may not be able to get you any land, but we will help get you another room."

"I'm not so sure about that," Bob said. "My case worker already found me two rooms and I blew it."

Five days later, Cathy showed up in her telephone booth and all was well in Bob's world again. One of the homeless agencies had put Cathy up in a hotel to help her recuperate. However, despite her days of luxurious living, Cathy was still coughing.

Bob ended up in the hospital twice more the following week, making a total of seven times since we'd met him. Even the normally robust and vibrant Tony had fallen down the subway stairs and broken his collarbone. His face was bruised, both eyes were black, and his right arm was in a sling.

The Fourth of July weekend was approaching. We were nervous to leave town even for a few days, but the city was insufferably hot, and we were both emotionally and physically drained. On July 2nd, we decided to make one last trip down Park Avenue to check on our friends before heading upstate.

To our relief, both Bob and Cathy were in their telephone booths. Cathy, however, was semi-conscious. Bob tried to wake her. Finally, I was able to get her to open her eyes for a few seconds before she drifted back to sleep.

We decided to hang out with Bob for a while in the hope that Cathy would wake up. An hour later, she opened her eyes and was in a foul mood.

"How are you feeling?" I asked.

"I'm still sick," she said, then started coughing violently. Bob looked over at her with alarm. I wondered whether she still had bronchitis or had finally caught COVID. I backed away.

"They gave me an antibiotic, but I think I need more."

"Who gave you an antibiotic? The hospital?"

"No, the drop-in center," she replied.

"Did anyone give you a COVID test?"

"Oh yeah, my fifth one. I told them idiots that I never had the virus, and if I hadn't gotten it by now, I wasn't going to get it."

"Maybe you should go ask for some more antibiotics?" I suggested.

Cathy nodded and stood up as if she was about to leave. Instead, she stopped in the middle of the street right behind the telephone booths, dropped her pants and urinated. It came down in a loud, continuous stream that sounded as if the fire hydrant had been opened. *Wow, she must not have relieved herself for a long time.* Bob heard the ruckus, turned around and saw the spectacle.

"Disgusting," he shouted with vehemence. "Right beside my telephone booth."

Cathy finished her business, pulled up her pants, came back and sat down next to Bob as if nothing had happened.

"Disgusting," he said a second time, staring in her direction. Cathy did not notice or pretended not to care.

"Why don't you go ask them if you can have some more medicine?" I said again.

"I'll go later, my friend is coming. Will you go buy me some pads?"

"Let's go together," I suggested. The nearest drug store was two blocks away. We walked in silence down Park Avenue, and I could tell something was weighing on her mind.

Cathy picked out some pads and cough syrup. We paid and left the store. She was unusually quiet. "I need to ask you something," she said.

"What do you need?"

"They told me in the hospital that I've got Hep-C, and I need someone to bury me if I die." I was so shocked that I surprised myself when my mouth started moving.

"You're not going to die, Cathy. There are drugs that can cure Hep-C." What I didn't say was that I also knew the price of those drugs was high. I wondered whether Medicaid would cover the cost of a prescription for her.

"Where can I get some?" she asked.

"Tell your case worker at Bellevue you need to see a doctor."

"Okay, I will," she said, and rummaged through her pockets and produced the business card of her case worker. I took a picture of her holding the card and then a close-up of the card itself so I could keep a copy in my photos.

We walked up Park Avenue, arms around each other like two school girls sharing secrets. People stared—two women, one white and middle-aged, the other Black, obviously homeless, and young. It was an intimate moment. We looked at each other and laughed. Neither of us said anything, but I had the distinct feeling we were both enjoying the confused glances of the people we passed.

When we got back to the telephone booths I decided to have Cathy write down what I had just suggested she tell her case worker at Bellevue.

"Do you have a piece of paper?" I asked. Cathy produced a scrap from her duffle bag and Joel handed her a pen. "Here, write this down. My name is Cathy. I have Hep-C and need to see a doctor." It took her five minutes to write those few words. She finally finished but not before Bob complained.

"What are you doing for God's sakes, writing a book?"

Cathy frowned at Bob and handed me the piece of paper to read. After confirming she had written everything down correctly, I gave it back to her.

"Good job! Give this to your Bellevue advocate next week." Cathy nodded, and put the paper back into her duffle bag. "In any event, don't worry. I'll make sure you're buried properly," I promised her. "But I'm almost thirty years older than you, Cathy, so odds are you will be coming to my funeral and not the other way around."

Cathy smiled. Even as I said it, I knew I was not being completely honest. Hep-C is a virus that attacks the liver and can be life-threatening if not treated properly. I thought about my cousin. He'd died from Hep-C and cirrhosis of the liver when he was fifty-eight. For now, however, Cathy was still alive and happy again.

I motioned to Joel that it was time to leave. We were almost home when I spotted Kyle panhandling at his usual post on 37th Street. When we stopped to give him a sandwich, it was clear he wasn't in good shape.

"My eyes are turning colors," he said.

"You mean you are seeing colors?" Joel asked.

"No, they are turning colors. Sometimes they are white, sometimes black, and sometimes red." I stared at his eyes. The only color I saw was the beautiful green of his irises.

Joel and I looked at each other. For a moment, neither of us spoke. Kyle's reports of visual and auditory hallucinations seemed to pale in comparison to his latest news.

"How do you know they are different colors?" I asked.

"I've seen them in the bathroom mirror," he replied. "And some of the people who live at the Andrews have seen them change colors, too."

"I'll send an email to Karen when I get home," I promised. "She'll make an appointment for you with an eye doctor."

Joel and I walked back to the apartment in silence, but when we were in the safety of our living room, I let it all out.

"I can't do this anymore," I confessed. "They're all drug addicts and criminals."

"You know we can't stop until we get them all off the streets, Trace, or they may die out there. Cathy and Tony don't even have case workers yet."

"Okay, but when we get back here next week, I'm taking a break."

"Fine, take a break," Joel agreed. "Are you ready to go up to Mahopac?"

"Yeah, let's get going."

We gathered our belongings, walked to the garage in silence, got into our car and headed upstate to our house on the lake where I felt we belonged.

■ — ■ — ■

Maggie Wright, July 2020

William had made the transition from living on the streets to living with him in Brooklyn easy. I was surprised at how quickly I was moving on, and not only moving on, but not looking back. Each day brought me further away from Rick. As the days passed, I grew happier and more secure in both my new home and my new relationship.

The first time I saw Rick after his release, when Henry was picked up to be taken to his safe haven room, my heart sank. I felt awful that I had abandoned him. I knew he expected me to be waiting on our street corner when he was released from jail. I know it hurt him deeply that I was not there and I felt guilty.

When I talked about my conflicted feelings with William, he was quick to remind me that Rick had been abusing me for years, and that this was my chance to have a fresh start. I knew he was right, but part of me wondered if I had moved on too quickly. I felt like I owed more to Rick than abandoning him when things got tough.

This gnawed at me for days, and I finally knew that I had to speak to Rick in private and clear the air. I told William that I was going to The Travelers to get some things and speak with my case worker. Instead, I went to Rick's spot to talk with him. I needed to explain that our breakup had been a long time coming, and that it was for the best.

Rick approached me and hugged me. He cried and told me he was sorry for all the times he had hurt me, and to please stay with him and give him another chance.

I hesitated. It was only for a moment, but I actually considered staying there on that street corner with him. I loved him. I didn't want to leave him, but there was really no choice. I was going to move forward with my relationship with William. Rick and I were finally done.

I disentangled myself from Rick's arms. "I still love you, but I can't deal with the abuse and misery of our relationship."

He listened in silence and then punched me in the face. When I fell on the sidewalk, he jumped on top of me and grabbed my purse, dumping everything out of it. He smashed my phone and kneed me in the ribs.

"I hope you die," he said, and then ran away before someone could report the beating. As I got up and gathered my destroyed things, I could feel my eye swelling. I knew William would be furious. I'd tried to make things better and instead made them worse.

When I arrived home, William took one look at me and started screaming. "I'm going to kill that bastard."

I didn't tell him that I had actively sought Rick out. Instead, I lied and said I'd run into him on the street. William was angry that I'd stopped to talk to Rick, but he was angrier that he hadn't been there to protect me. He told me that no man, especially Rick, would ever lay a hand on me again. This broke my heart. William had done nothing wrong. I had. Yet, William was blaming himself for the fiasco I'd created.

With William, I felt safe and loved for the first time in a very long time. But I couldn't rid myself of a nagging thought.

Did I deserve it?

CHAPTER 11

Fluid Truth

—————■—————

Our restorative escape from the city over the long Fourth of July weekend was muted by our growing suspicion that Mark was using drugs again. He called Joel several times asking for money, and Joel wired it to him via Western Union. I voiced what I knew Joel was thinking.

"I don't understand how it's possible that he needs so much money when he has no rent or food expenses?"

"He says he can't eat the food at The Travelers."

"Well, he was paying for food when he was living in his apartment in Harlem, so why doesn't he just buy some?"

"I know, Trace, I think he's started using again. I'm not sending him another dime."

I texted Maggie and asked if she could keep an eye out for Mark. Maggie, per usual, was eager to pay it forward. She routinely spent her mornings checking on the people in our group when we were not in the city. Asking her to check up on Mark was an assignment she gladly accepted.

Maggie took her responsibility seriously and brought a special sort of enthusiasm to her unofficial role. Being formerly homeless, she knew the difficulty of the streets. She also knew the tricks and the games. No one got away with anything on Maggie's watch.

However, Maggie was still very much a woman in transition herself. Basic things that we take for granted like going to bed at night and waking up in the morning instead of cat-napping during the day have to be relearned by homeless people once they become sheltered. This process could take months.

Another thing they have to overcome is the temptation to relieve themselves on the streets. One morning, Maggie hid behind a bush in the middle of Madison Square Park, dropped her pants, and urinated. William took her picture and was quick to show it to me thinking it was funny.

"Listen," I said, pulling her aside. "Keep your pants on until you are in a private place." I purposely kept my advice light so Maggie would "hear" it. I'd learned that Maggie, as well as most of the homeless people we'd met, shut down their emotions quickly at the slightest sign of disapproval. My ruse worked. She started laughing hysterically. To my knowledge, she never urinated in public again.

Despite our growing concern over Mark's possible renewed drug use, the weather was gorgeous over the weekend. Our son, daughter and her family were with us in Mahopac and life felt normal for a few days. Dozens of boats with scores of happy people were in full view, a stark contrast to the faceless sidewalks of Manhattan.

We returned to the city on Tuesday morning, made the sandwiches, and set out. We found Kyle on his corner. He was still not doing well. At this point, however, we had become somewhat inured to the constant fluctuations in his mood and behavior. Like the rest of us, he had good days and bad. When I asked him how he was doing, his usual response was, "miserable as always."

I started to wonder what might change the dynamics for Kyle. I decided it was time to broach the subject of his heroin addiction.

"Kyle, I don't want to tell you how to live your life, but can't you get a prescription to control your back pain? Just think of what you could do with the money you make panhandling if you did not have to spend it all on heroin."

Kyle looked down the street with a pensive expression on his face. It was the first time I confronted him about his heroin addiction. "I've been thinking about that a lot lately, and I've decided I'm going into treatment as soon as my Medicaid card arrives."

At this point, I should have said something like, "great news," but instead I pushed him harder. "Do you have to wait until you get the card? You have your Medicaid account number. Isn't that enough?"

"I want my card."

I really should have backed off then. Instead, I blundered again. "You know, Kyle, only you can turn your life around. You have the chance to take all your pain and suffering and transform it into a powerful tool to help others. It's up to you."

Kyle appeared to agree with me, yet when he spoke, all he said was, "I have to synthesize what you just said."

"Okay. I'm not going to bug you any more about this today. The last thing I'm going to say is that you always tell me you are on the streets because you want to be free. You may be free from society, but you are a slave to heroin."

Kyle looked off into the distance again and nodded then turned and looked directly into my eyes. "You're right. I'm not really free because heroin is my master."

In addition to being smart, Kyle had a photographic memory and was able to remember details of his life that I wouldn't be able to do even if I kept a daily journal. He was also a walking encyclopedia when it came to medical conditions and the drugs that treated them. For example, Kyle knew he could control his back pain with a combination of buprenorphine and gabapentin. This made it even more difficult for me to accept his heroin use. I had to face the truth—Kyle was in an advanced stage of addiction and far more likely than not to die from it.

I dropped the subject of his heroin addiction and we said goodbye and headed downtown to check on Bob and Cathy, who, as usual, were stationed in their telephone booths.

"Someone has a birthday coming up," Joel said, as we arrived.

"Yes, it's this Saturday," Bob replied, smiling brightly. "I'll be six-ty-five."

"What do you want for your birthday?" Joel asked.

Bob looked surprised though he wasted no time in answering Joel's question.

"I need me a haircut and a beard trim so I look nice for my birth-day."

"Come on, then, let's go to the barbershop right now," Joel offered.

"Nah, I can't walk that far right now."

We knew better than to give him money having learned the hard way from Joel's experience with Mark that handing out significant amounts of cash was not a good idea, as it was invariably used to buy drugs or alcohol. Ironically, small amounts of money were far more likely to be used for food or for purchases at McDonald's in order to use the bathroom.

"Call me later if you feel like going," Joel offered. Bob never called.

Cathy was not doing well either, and we started wondering if she was using crack. Up until that point, as far as we knew, she was only either drinking vodka or smoking pot. However, since her Hep-C diagnosis, she was just not the same—her attitude felt defeatist. Before her diagnosis, I'd been able to easily elicit a smile from Cathy. Now, she more often exhibited a brashness and lack of gratitude, which I found increasingly problematic. When I handed her five dollars, she frowned.

"What about the money for the days you weren't here?" she asked.

I was flabbergasted but decided to make a joke out of it. "You want back pay?"

To her credit, Cathy laughed even though she continued to pout. Nevertheless, there was good news for her that day—after twenty years of homelessness, she'd finally been assigned a case worker, leaving only Tony without one.

The next morning, Maggie's mother called me for the first time. I'd been in routine email contact with her since she'd written to thank me for the books, but we'd not yet spoken on the phone. So I was surprised when my phone rang, and her name appeared on my caller ID.

"Hi, Traci, it's Maggie's mother" she said. "I thought I should call you concerning your email about Maggie's brother having sent her money."

"Yes, wasn't that so nice of him?"

"Traci, I don't know how to tell you this, which is the reason for my call. Maggie does not have a brother. She has one sister who lives on Staten Island."

"But she said that her father was married before. Maybe she was talking about a son he'd had with his first wife?"

"No, it's true that he was married before, but his only children are our two daughters."

"Maybe his first wife had a son? Maybe Maggie meant her step-brother?"

"No, Traci, Maggie's father's first wife never had any children."

"Why would Maggie tell me a story about a brother—she said his name was Bryan—who lives in California?"

"I really don't know, Traci, and I am sorry to have to say this. Maggie does not always tell the truth."

My heart sank. What else wasn't true? I decided the best way to find out was to ask Maggie. When I ran into her later that day, I wasted no time. "Hey, your mom called and said you don't have a brother?"

"Oh, that doesn't matter," Maggie said, waving her hand in the air as if she were swatting away a fly. "Bryan was the first person who helped me when I was on the street. He calls me his sister, and I call him my brother."

"Oh, that makes sense," I said, relieved. "Do you mind giving me his email and cell phone number so I can contact him in case of an emergency?" To my amazement, Maggie shared Bryan's contact information.

"Tell me about him, please," I asked. Maggie's face lit up.

"Oh, he's just the best," she gushed. "He used to live and work here in the city right around the corner. In the winter, he went out to California and checked himself into an alcohol treatment center. Before he left, he gave me $500 and told me he'd be back in touch when his thirty-day program ended."

"Did he come back yet?"

"No, he found a girlfriend out there and is relocating. I'm so glad for him, but I'm sure going to miss him. He used to come by our corner every day and give me a few dollars and some food."

I went back to my apartment that afternoon convinced that Maggie's use of the word "brother" was not a lie. Relief arrived until I spoke with Maggie's mother for a second time later that night.

I knew Maggie was a voracious reader. We'd had any number of conversations about this or that book, and she was always asking to borrow ones that I was reading when I finished them. The first book I lent her was over four hundred pages and I was sure I'd never see it again. To my utter astonishment, she returned it less than twenty-four hours later.

At some point, I'd started considering writing this book about my experience helping the homeless during the pandemic. I was thinking of offering Maggie a job as my developmental editor. While I'd been on the streets for four months and had learned quite a bit about homelessness, she had lived on them for three years and knew far more about the subject and the people than I did. Later that evening, I called Maggie's mother to discuss my plan.

"I'm thinking about writing a book, and I'm considering offering Maggie a job as a developmental editor. She seems very well-read, and she does have a college degree, so I'm assuming she can work on written materials."

"Traci, Maggie does not have a college degree."

"Wait," I interrupted her, "Maggie told me she has a graduate degree in psychology." At this, Maggie's mother started laughing so loudly I thought she might pee her pants.

"A graduate degree?" she asked in disbelief. "No, Maggie does not have a graduate degree. In fact, she dropped out of college."

"Why would she do that?"

"A boy—the scum of the earth—she spent all her time with him. When she flunked her statistics class, she just gave up."

"That's really too bad," I said. "She is smart and very well-read."

"You're right about that. And she had 119 credits and a 3.4 GPA. All she needed to graduate was to pass that statistics class. As you said, Maggie is a voracious reader and an excellent writer. She should have studied English in college, but she wanted to study psychology."

"Well, do you think she could do a good job working as my developmental editor anyway?"

"Yes, Traci, I believe she would do a good job with an assignment like that."

Comforted by the reassurance, and despite my unease about Maggie's tendency to lie, the next morning, I spoke with her about the book.

"I'm thinking about writing a book about homelessness and the pandemic. Would you like to work on it?"

"Yes!" she shouted and started jumping up and down.

What I didn't ask her, however, what I simply could not bring myself to ask that morning, was why she'd told me she had a graduate degree. Nevertheless, I did confront her about some of the other things her mother had shared with me, primarily, Maggie's drinking and opioid use and the theft she'd engaged in to support both habits. Maggie owned up to everything.

"I never said I was a perfect person. You know how I got addicted to opioids—that root canal. Then I used vodka to get off the drugs."

"Yeah, I know you told me this before. You didn't tell me you stole money from your family to buy them."

Despite her bravado, I could tell Maggie was uncomfortable with the discussion. Although I am not a particularly religious person, I decided to tell her a Bible story.

"I know you're Jewish, but have you ever heard the story about Jesus and the woman who was caught in the act of adultery?"

"I think I have heard something about that," she said. "Can you tell me the story anyway?"

"A woman was caught with a man who was not her husband and was brought to Jesus. The gathering crowd asked Jesus to confirm that stoning was the punishment for adultery at the time."

"And?" she asked.

"Jesus agreed that the punishment for adultery was indeed stoning and then suggested that the person in the crowd who was without sin should throw the first stone."

"Who threw the first stone?" she asked.

"Nobody, or so the story goes." Maggie seemed to understand the point of the story and smiled. "From now on, whenever one of us does something that is less than Kosher, we'll just say, *the first stone.*"

"I like that!" Maggie exclaimed.

Later that morning, we ran into Bob, who was beside himself because Cathy was missing again. I decided it was time to ask the question we'd all been avoiding.

"Do you think she is using drugs? Something other than smoking pot?"

Bob lowered his head. "Yes, I think she is using crack, and she stole all my money last night."

"How did she do that?" Joel asked.

"I was drunk," Bob admitted, reaching behind his back for his not-so-hidden bottle of vodka.

"Oh, no," I said. "Maggie said crack is really expensive, and the high only lasts for seconds."

"Yep," Bob confirmed.

Bob was in a foul mood over his birthday, as well as his stolen money. He'd expected his mother to make a dinner and cake and to invite his brother, cousins, nephews and nieces over to her apartment.

"None of that happened," he said. "My mom was sick and there was no dinner. No one even showed up."

"Man, I'm so sorry, Bob," Joel said.

Changing the subject, he said, "I need a pair of jeans. The mosquitoes are biting my legs at night." I was surprised to hear that there were mosquitoes in the city. I'd never seen any. Then again, I'd never slept on the streets.

Joel raised another issue. "We just bought you a pair of jeans last month. Where are they?"

"They were stolen from my room at The Andrews," Bob replied.

"I thought the rooms were all locked and each one had a secure dresser?" Joel said.

"Yes, they do, but someone came into my room using the fire escape while I was taking a shower and stole my pants right off the bed. That's one of the reasons I did not want to go back there."

We said we'd get him another pair, but something was nagging me. I suspected that Bob was lying to us about his jeans. But why?

The next day, Bob's cousin was visiting when we arrived. We'd met him several times before that day and found him to be an agreeable young man. The first thing he blurted out caused us concern.

"Bob's mom made him the best strawberry shortcake for his birthday. It was delicious!"

Joel looked at Bob who stared at his cousin with such a penetrating gaze that I thought he might jump up from his chair and tackle him.

"He got some nice gifts, too," he added.

"What gifts?" Joel asked, surprised.

"Two pairs of nice jeans!"

It was too much for us to process standing there on the street and, not wanting to confront Bob in front of his cousin, we handed out the sandwiches and said we had an appointment downtown.

Joel and I walked to Union Square in silence. I wondered whether we were both thinking the same thing. Why would Bob lie about his jeans and birthday cake? One thing was true, however. Cathy had not gone with Bob to his house for his birthday as planned, and we all wondered where she had been that day. No one knew what was up with Cathy. But the following day, we did learn the reason Bob kept asking for jeans—he'd started losing control of his bowels.

Two days later, Cathy was sitting next to Bob in the telephone booth as if nothing had happened.

"Where have you been, Cathy?" I asked.

"I'm in trouble," she said.

"You mean because of your Hep-C?" I asked. She answered with a complete non sequitur.

"I don't want to go back to that jail again."

"Again?" I asked. The only two people we thought had *not* been in jail were Maggie and Cathy.

"I was convicted of twenty felonies and went to prison a few years ago."

"How many years were you there?" Joel asked.

"Two long years. Prison is no place to be."

"What were you convicted of?" I asked.

"Don't really know. Stealing. Drugs. Other stuff. They bunched all twenty felonies together."

"What prison were you in?" I asked.

"The Edna. Over in New Jersey."

The Edna Mahan Correctional Facility for Women was located in Clinton, New Jersey. Later that evening, Joel and I looked it up on Google. The prison housed approximately one thousand female convicts. In April 2020, the US Department of Justice had released a report detailing the open secret of sexual misconduct committed by the guards.

Neither of us asked Cathy for further details about her convictions that morning—somehow, it just didn't matter. Cathy had been sexually abused by her father and stepfather, and possibly, by some of the guards in that prison. She had Hep-C. And now it appeared likely that she was smoking crack.

We were despondent, no longer able to emotionally separate ourselves from Cathy's struggles, or those of any of our homeless friends. Their suffering impacted us. Once strangers to be feared, they had become part of us. The lines of demarcation blurred, making us more and more empathetic—and also, more vulnerable.

How did I get myself into this mess? The homeless men and women in our neighborhood had evolved from strangers who we perceived as objects to be avoided, to people with names and stories, to friends, albeit with sordid backgrounds laden with incarcerations and drug addictions. Somehow, it no longer mattered. Most notably, it was now clear to me that we loved them.

All of them.

■ – ■ – ■

Maggie Wright, July 2020

One of the hardest parts about being homeless is that you lose your identity. The moment you sit on a corner with a cup in your hand, people actively go out of their way to avoid looking at you. On the one hand, you don't want to be noticed; most days, you prefer to fade into the background. However, for some of the homeless people, retaining a part of who they used to be is necessary to make it through the day.

I was a mixture of both. Part of me wanted to disappear off the planet and never look or speak to anyone again. The other part of me was dying to reclaim part of who I used to be, believing that if I could, maybe there was still hope for me. I was cautious of everyone and guarded of my past.

My way of handling that was to become the intelligent homeless woman. The smart one. Some people stopped to ask questions about The New York Times crossword puzzle on their way into the office. I was the one with the graduate degree in psychology who had fallen on hard times. Of course, this was not true.

While I am smart and can finish the crossword puzzle in under thirty minutes, I also did not have a graduate degree, or even an undergraduate one. Psych statistics had done me in. So did spending all those days with my boyfriend when I should have been in school. I was one semester away from graduating. Wasn't that close enough? What harm could it do to tell people that I had a degree? I just needed their help, and, most of them, I would never see again. It was just a little white lie, right?

This theory went out the window after I met Traci. Introducing Traci to my mother was a huge deal for me for many reasons. One, of course, was combining the two worlds—who I used to be before I was homeless, and who I was now. For the first time, I really had to confront the two, and it was very sobering for me.

The other problem was that I knew I'd told Traci things that were not true and that my mother would tell her the truth if the subject ever came up. I was afraid that if she did, I might lose Traci's friendship. But truths and lies have a way of meshing together on the sidewalk. I couldn't even remember all the things I'd been dishonest about.

Then one morning, which I will never forget, Traci asked me if I would be interested in working as a developmental editor for a book she was thinking of writing about her experience with the homeless people of New York City. I wanted to burst into tears—actually I think I did. Someone thought I could work for them. Someone still believed in me! Then, came the fear. Was she offering me this because she thought I was a college graduate? What would happen if she asked for proof of my degree?

I was desperate to prove that I was still worth something. After Traci left, I called my mother to tell her that Traci thought I would be a good fit to *work as an editor on her next book. I fessed up to my mom and told her that I had lied to Traci about being a college graduate.*

My mother asked me why I'd done this, and I could tell from her tone that she was about to let me have it. I couldn't blame her. I knew my mother hated it when I lied. In a desperate attempt to avoid the inevitable, I recounted the story from the Bible that Traci told me. My mother listened in silence. At first, I thought she might be mad that I'd told her a story about Jesus because we're Jewish. But then she surprised me.

"Don't mess this up, Maggie. You are capable of doing a very good job with this assignment. Don't let us down. Don't let yourself down."

CHAPTER 12

Mothering

———■———

The relationship between Maggie and her mother was complicated, as many mother-daughter relationships can be. Maggie wanted to see her children. Her mother was anxious that she do so. Months went by, and Maggie and her mother grew frustrated and started snipping at one another.

"My mom thinks I can just get on a bus and show up at the house to see the children. I just can't do that," Maggie complained.

"It's only natural that your mom is anxious about this," I said.

"True, but what can I do?"

I had not yet mentioned anything about my mother to Maggie. Her mother had her faults, as we all do, but Maggie found any excuse to blame her mother for her own misfortune. I knew this habit well—for many years, I'd blamed my mother for everything that had gone wrong in my life. I realized now was the time to tell Maggie the truth.

"You know what they say, right?" I asked, in an effort to broach the subject.

"What?" she said, hands on hips and jaw jutted forward, a clear indication that she was not inclined to listen to one of my feel-good lectures.

"We're all victims of victims."

"Well, that's easy for you to say. I bet your mom was great. I bet she told you she loved you every single day."

"Do you have a minute?" I asked. "Let me tell you a story."

■ – ■ – ■

June 1978. "I just want you to remember one thing," my mother said.

"What's that, Mom?"

"No matter what happens, I love you."

It was the first and only time she said those three words to me. Maybe there were other times she told me in a different way. Like the time when I was in the fifth grade, and she told me to move my little leg away from the table she was dusting, so there would be no risk of a falling object hurting me. I could feel her love in those words.

I remember the time as a teenager when she hid a hundred dollar bill in my Valentine's Day chocolate candy and was so pleased when I found it. And I remember the time my brother and I walked back from school and found her waiting on our front porch with homemade chocolate-chip cookies and lemonade. But I don't remember any other time she said *I love you* other than the evening of June 25th, 1978.

It was six weeks before my wedding. Joel and I were living with his parents in Westchester, New York. We'd already found our first apartment in Brooklyn. Our parents advised us not to move into it, however, until after the wedding. Appearances were still important forty years ago.

I should have known something was wrong. I should have called back and spoken to my father. I didn't.

I was the lucky one that night. Her favorite child, my brother, Jeff, heard something quite different that evening. He would tell me the next morning that the last words he heard were, "Go to bed—you will have a long day tomorrow."

He always blamed himself for doing what she said. "I should have stayed up. I should have put her to bed."

After Jeff fell asleep, our mother must have slipped into her bedroom and taken off her wedding rings, leaving them on the nightstand next to her side of the bed—my father's first clue that something was amiss when he woke up the following morning.

When the phone rang at seven o'clock in Joel's parents' house, I knew my life was about to change irrevocably. There is something about early morning phone calls that alert our senses to bad news. I felt it on a cellular level. The hair on my arms stood straight up and adrenaline started pumping through my body. Just like that morning in Turks, I wanted to run but couldn't. I picked up the phone extension in my bedroom instead. It was my brother.

"Rug is dead." Rug. My brother had given our mother that nickname towards the end of her life because she'd cut her hair short, causing it to sort of sit on top of her head like a rug. "Rug is dead," he repeated in a tone devoid of any perceptible feeling. He'd been living at home that summer. Had he suspected something this awful might happen or, like me, was he in shock?

I could not utter the simplest response. My racing mind at last fixed itself on the needs of my brother and dad. When I finally spoke, all I said was, "I will be on the next plane to DC." Then I dropped the phone and started screaming.

Within an hour, Joel and I were sitting on an airplane. When we emerged in the arrival lounge, I spotted my father and brother, confused and disheveled. Joel offered to drive, and my father nodded his agreement. On our way to my grandmother's house, my father told us what had happened. Jeff sat motionless beside him, staring straight ahead.

When he'd found my mother's wedding rings on the nightstand beside their bed, he'd gone in search of her. I imagined him stumbling through the house, still half asleep in his old pajama bottoms, hair uncombed, glasses askew. Our mother wasn't in the bathroom, or in the kitchen preparing coffee, or in the den watching the morning news. Then, he caught a whiff of carbon monoxide. The deadly gas, at first odorless, had become nauseating overnight and drew his attention to our attached garage, located just off the den. My father opened the door and descended the three steps to the gray cement floor. The southern sun was already making its presence felt through the side window, despite the early hour. My father almost fainted from the combination of heat, gasoline, and carbon monoxide fumes. He rushed to the garage door and flung it open to let the fresh air in.

He stepped outside and called her name. She wasn't in the garden or on the patio.

"I already knew where she was," my father told us. "I just couldn't bring myself to look inside the car yet."

He returned to the garage and walked back up the three stairs to our den, turning his head around one last time to see if maybe she was coming down the street. And then he allowed himself to look inside the car.

He opened the driver's side door and reached in. Her lifeless body, already cold but strangely peaceful, was lying on the front seat—the front seat of the same car I would soon ride in to the church to be married. I never asked why we used that car. It was our only car, but we could have borrowed my grandmother's. At the time, however, it did not even occur to me that it was odd.

My father lifted my mother's thin body off of the front seat, brought her into the house, and laid her on the couch in our living room. Despite the June heat, he covered her with her favorite blanket.

He then descended to my brother's bedroom in our finished basement. Jeff was in the shower—a spiral-shaped shell that needed no door. My dad poked his head in and around the first curve, and before Jeff could register that my dad's head had suddenly appeared under the same running water as his own, my father delivered the news that would shatter Jeff's life. He was nineteen-years-old.

"Your mom is dead."

Jeff stepped out, leaving the water running, and grabbed a towel. My father told me that Jeff's chin shifted unnaturally from left to right as if it had been knocked out of its proper location. My brother tied the towel around his waist and, and still dripping water, went upstairs to the kitchen to call me.

My dad was still telling us the story when we pulled into my grandmother's driveway just after ten a.m. When the four of us walked into her kitchen, she was drinking her morning coffee and reading the newspaper at the table. She stood up and stumbled backwards, a questioning look on her face, morphing into alarm. I thought for a chilling second that we might lose her too.

My father wasted no time in delivering the news we all knew would devastate her.

"Jean killed herself last night, Minnie." He used my grandmother's nickname, given to her due to her shortness.

My grandmother's face twisted into unnatural opposing directions. She fell to the ground and, pounding the kitchen floor with her clenched fists, screamed. "Not my Jean!"

The next few days were a blur as we scurried to make funeral arrangements for a woman who did not yet have a burial plot. We decided to bury her in my grandmother's still-unused one.

I don't remember a single word that was spoken at the gravesite. When the service ended, I stood up and took a white rose from atop my mother's casket and walked away. As I approached the waiting funeral car, I stopped and smelled the rose. Then I dropped it in the gutter. I did not look back as my mother's casket was lowered into the ground. And I never cried a single tear.

Not one.

Instead, I started running away from myself. And I did not stop for forty years. And when I finally stopped, I found a woman who appeared to be in full control of her life but was shattered on the inside.

My mother did not leave a note. I never wondered why. What could she have said?

Maggie looked at me as I finished my story, mouth open, tears running down her face.

"Whose mother kills herself six weeks before her daughter's wedding?"

"My mother," I whispered.

I stood on Park Avenue staring at Maggie who was staring at me. Two women—one broken and afraid, the other broken and defiant. As I walked away it occurred to me that I did not know who was who.

It also occurred to me that I loved my mother. I'd wasted an entire life denying this truth in some misguided belief that pretending that I didn't care would protect me from the pain of her loss.

■ – ■ – ■

MAGGIE WRIGHT, JULY 2020

My mother and I didn't speak a single word to one another for the first two and a half years I was on the street. I don't think she even knew where I was.

I might never have spoken to her again, had it not been for her friend's husband happening upon me one afternoon as I was panhandling. Our eyes locked. I don't know who was more horrified—him seeing me begging on the sidewalk, or me seeing a vestige of my past life standing in front of me. It was the first time anyone I'd known from my past life had seen me panhandling. I decided it was best to give my mother a call before she heard the news from her friend.

Surprisingly enough, at first, my mother seemed happy to hear from me. Then she told me how disappointed she was that I'd disappeared from my children's lives and become a homeless alcoholic. I explained to her what I'd endured in the past years, but she didn't want to hear about it. All she cared about was me getting back to my children.

One morning, I was feeling particularly hurt by the last conversation I'd with her, and I told Traci as much. That is when she told me about her mother.

I had always assumed Traci had come from a wonderful, loving family. I believed she must have had a solid foundation to become so successful. One day, she stopped me mid-sentence when I was complaining, and she told me a story that forever changed the way I looked at her...and myself.

As I stood there listening to Traci tell me about her mother's suicide, my mind found it impossible to believe, or grasp, the enormity of what she was saying. I couldn't stop the tears from flowing.

I suddenly felt extremely shallow. Here I was complaining to Traci about my mother "not being nice to me" and "being too hard on me." Meanwhile, Traci didn't even have a mother to complain about. I stood on that corner feeling an anger that is hard to describe. My head started throbbing, and my hands involuntarily clenched into fists. Then I felt guilty and started crying even harder.

William was surprised to see so much raw emotion in me. My mother was alive, and she hadn't given up on me yet. Despite everything. She was still rooting for me.

Traci gave me an invaluable gift that day. She made me realize that my situation was my fault, and mine alone. That was the first day that I stopped pointing my finger at my mother, at Rick, at the world. Instead, I started pointing my finger at myself.

CHAPTER 13

Y Shelter?

———■———

The disproportionate financial hardship caused by the pandemic continued to niggle at me. The restaurant business was struggling to survive, the public transportation system was laying off workers by the hundreds due to a lack of riders, and the hair and nail salons were empty.

While the traffic in the city was noticeably heavier after the Phase Three reopening began on July 6th, the homeless were still struggling to collect even ten dollars a week. The have-and-have-not divide that had already been defining the country for years was widening.

In 2011 there were 42,190 homeless people in New York City and the Dow Jones ended the year at 12,217.56. By the end of 2019, the number of homeless exceeded 70,000, and the Dow closed at 29,538.44. Even the early losses the Dow experienced in March and April, causing the rich to bemoan their misfortunes, were all but recovered by July. A year later, the Dow would close at over 35,000 while the homeless population had soared.

Meanwhile, in sharp contrast to the brokerage account gains enjoyed by the most fortunate, *The New York Times* reported that there had been a new surge in unemployment claims for the first time in four months. Another 975,000 workers had also filed for the $600 additional weekly benefit, offered through the federal unemployment program.

The *New York Times* article also reported a further distressing statistic from a survey conducted by the Census Bureau: "The discouraging news from the Labor Department followed a Census Bureau survey showing that four million fewer people were employed last week than the week before. It was the fourth straight decline, suggesting that nearly all the job gains since mid-May had been erased."

Gregory Daco, chief U.S. economist at Oxford Economics, confirmed what I noticed in the city's restaurants, hair and nail salons and on buses and subways—that while these businesses had been allowed to reopen, there was a significant decrease in demand for their services.

The *Times* reported that 30 million people—roughly one in five American workers—were receiving jobless benefits. This number would not have included the stylists I saw sitting in their empty chairs, the hundreds of servers I saw standing outside wearing masks and gloves, hoping that a few pedestrians would stop to eat lunch or dinner in the beautifully-adorned outside dining spaces, and certainly not the undocumented immigrants in the nail salons or restaurant kitchens who loaded a smattering of dirty dishes into empty, industrial-sized dishwashing machines.

Due to expire at the end of the month was the Federal Paycheck Protection Program, the benefit program my friend Jan was never able to procure for her restaurant, which provided small businesses with emergency loans. Nevertheless, Republicans continued to battle amongst themselves over what to do next, rather than putting forward a proposal for negotiating with the Democrats. As the expiration date drew near, little progress was made.

I wondered how many more homeless people would appear on the city streets before the pandemic was over. There was still a moratorium on evictions, but sooner or later, it would be lifted. In the meantime, many landlords, now with a plethora of non-paying tenants occupying their buildings, were struggling to pay their mortgages and taxes. As a result, many had simply walked away from their properties, losing their entire investments in the process. I couldn't help but wonder which was worse for landlords—a glut of empty apartments or the units with non-paying tenants who were protected from eviction.

The saddest financial story for me personally was learning that some of my homeless friends were selling their monthly allotment of food stamps for sixty cents on the dollar. I overheard Maggie telling Kyle that she could get him ninety cents on the dollar through a source she and William had found in Brooklyn, causing Kyle to shout out in excitement. I reflected on the difficulty of finding a solution that would ensure the homeless use their food stamps for food.

Everywhere I looked, it was another Hobson's choice—a situation in which there are no good options.

Unable to do very much to help the millions of unemployed New Yorkers, we redoubled our efforts to alleviate the suffering of the few people we felt we could help. With money coming in from the GoFundMe page, we bought our homeless friends tee shirts, shorts, and sneakers.

Mark continued to ask Joel for extra money, and our fear that he was using drugs again was confirmed by Maggie when she reported seeing his stash of crack and hearing him boast that he'd bought it for $800. That news put an end to Joel's generosity—he vowed not to give Mark another dollar nor any items that could be sold or traded for drugs. Maybe it was just a coincidence, but it seemed that Mark went downhill as soon as his financial difficulties were alleviated.

"I think the extra money is what led him back to using crack," I said.

"I think you may be right, Trace. When he had to pay rent, he did not have any extra money to buy drugs. The only thing keeping him clean was the fear of being homeless again."

"I agree. What a shame. I really thought he had a chance to start a new life."

Mark was not the only one who used money to buy drugs. Kyle spent all of his money on heroin. Bob spent most of his money on vodka, Tony drank his share of vodka too, and Cathy smoked pot. Henry and Rick smoked K2 every chance they got. Even William and Maggie spent a good portion of their money on pot or K2. When I finally told them I would not give them any more money because it just went to buy K2, William said, "Thank God someone cares enough about us to even notice."

Despite the unwelcome news about Mark, there was some progress with Tony that week. He was finally assigned a case worker, Janet. Tony was the last person in our little group to get one. Within a few weeks, Janet offered him a safe haven room in Brooklyn. Unfortunately, Tony could not accept it because of his work schedule at the bodega in Manhattan. Janet promised to look for another room closer to where he worked.

Cathy's case worker also offered her a room in the Bronx. Likewise, she declined it due to its location. Our frustration and sense of hopelessness increased.

"They are surprisingly picky for people who have been sleeping on the sidewalk for years," I said to Joel.

"Yeah, but Tony really does need to be in Manhattan because of his job, and Cathy is not leaving Bob," Joel said.

Surprisingly, Rick, despite his arrest, was offered a room at The Andrews, and he gratefully accepted it. Rick appeared to be doing well. Maggie had seen him on the street several times and reported he looked better than ever.

"William and I walked right by Rick yesterday," she said. "He was unrecognizable—showered, clean clothes, shaven."

"I still can't believe Rick got a room with his recent arrest," I said.

"Me neither, but I'm glad for him. He needed a break."

"Yeah, I agree. Let's hope he can keep his nose clean," I said. I wasn't at all sure that he could.

My fear was confirmed on August 3rd when Maggie sent a photo of Rick, hands behind his back in handcuffs, having been detained by police on Lexington Avenue. He'd been caught wielding his pipe at a taxicab driver. Someone needs to take that pipe away from him, I thought.

Later that night Maggie called to tell me that the police had taken Rick to the hospital for a psych evaluation, rather than to police headquarters. He was evaluated and released.

"Why in the world would they do that?" I asked.

"I have no idea, Tray. They evaluated him and determined he was not in need of mental counseling and released him."

"If Rick doesn't need mental counseling, then I don't know who does," I said.

"I agree. Who knows what the truth is. All we know for sure is that he's back on the streets. And he still has his pipe."

The downward spiral continued the following day. Mark called, claiming that he'd been hospitalized and diagnosed with stomach cancer. He begged us for money for his medicine. Joel declined, knowing that the story wasn't true, and even if it was, Mark was on Medicaid and would have been entitled to receive whatever medicine he needed for free.

When this ruse did not work, Mark tried another story—he told Joel he had broken his parole and needed to report back to jail to finish his remaining ninety days.

"I need money to buy drugs to take to jail with me," he said.

Joel was flabbergasted and could not muster a coherent reply other than, "Sorry, man, I can't help you with that."

Later that afternoon we ran into William and Maggie, and I asked William about taking drugs into jail.

"Mark said that he plans to smuggle drugs into jail when he reports back to his parole officer. Can this be true?"

"Yeah."

"How would he get them inside?"

"Up his butt," William replied, matter-of-factly.

"I thought they searched up there?" I asked in a likewise matter-of-fact tone.

"Well, not exactly up his butt. He'd swallow them in a balloon, then poop them out a few days later."

It was all too much for me to absorb that afternoon standing on the sidewalk in the blazing heat. I decided to clear my head by taking a brisk walk to the grocery store. We needed some more bread and peanut butter for sandwiches.

It was a mistake.

While the brisk walk to the grocery store produced the outcome I craved, the return trip undid all its benefits.

As I approached the corner and waited for the green light, I spotted a woman and her small dachshund puppy across the street. When the walk sign started blinking, we both began crossing the street towards one another. Suddenly, a taxicab driver sped through the red light and hit her dog.

The dog started yelping.

The woman started screaming.

I ran across the street and dropped to my knees in the middle of Lexington Avenue. A caravan of speeding cars approached us. I knew the woman would not want to move her dog, so I stood and flapped my arms up and down to ward off the oncoming traffic. The woman sat in the middle of Lexington Avenue trembling. I recognized it as the same shock I'd experienced a few years earlier when our little dachshund, Dyllie, had been killed on the same corner. I also recognized the same lifeless gaze emanating from her dog's eyes.

A few minutes later the woman's husband arrived, panting profusely. He had the same dazed look on his face as his wife. Amazingly, he did the same thing Joel had done—he took off his shirt, knelt to the ground, and gently wrapped it around his dog. When they were safely off the street, I left. Meanwhile, my mind was spinning with memories of the day we lost our Dyllie.

■ – ■ – ■

February 2017. The weather was uncharacteristically warm. The apartment windows were open. The restaurants had set up tables outside even though the warm spell was predicted to last only a few days. New Yorkers are not known to miss an opportunity to have fun.

Joel was walking our two dogs—our yellow lab, Ellie, and Dyllie. I was in the living room painting the fireplace mantle when I heard an unnatural sound coming from outside. Thinking that someone had fallen on the street outside our window, I put my paint brush in the bucket and poked my head out the window to investigate.

The strange sound got louder, then faded. I hoped it was over. I then heard the elevator in the common area outside of our apartment door open. Joel burst through the door, screaming.

"Dyllie is dead. I have to go back. Here, watch Ellie."

Joel dropped our lab's leash and bolted back out the door. Ellie's head tilted to one side, as if she were trying to understand what had happened.

"Everything will be okay," I said. Ellie whimpered.

I ran out the door without shoes or coat, reaching the end of our street in less than ten seconds. Busy pedestrians had ceased their Saturday errands and were gathered on the corner. Cars and buses sped by unaware of the spectacle, creating a cascading river of shapes and colors. The omnipresent noise of New York City traffic muted, as my full attention was drawn to a single spot on Lexington Avenue.

Dyllie, our little dachshund was lying by the curb—still, silent, peaceful—almost as if she were sleeping. I crouched down and touched her head. She was still warm. I moved my hand to her chest and searched for a heartbeat.

Nothing.

I stood up, my hand covered in a warm, dripping, liquid. Someone from the gathering crowd yelled.

"She'll be okay. She'll be okay. Let's get her to the emergency hospital."

For a moment, I was encouraged by the stranger's optimism, until reality invaded the moment, stealing my fragile hope. A torrent of red, thick liquid—the same that covered my hand—began to leak from the corners of Dyllie's closed mouth and spread in an amoeba-like fashion across the blackness, creating a Jackson Pollack painting on the street.

Joel took off his sweatshirt, picked Dyllie up, and lovingly wrapped her inside the soft cloth. We ran down the middle of Lexington Avenue. Two glass-eyed people, one of us shoeless and howling, the other carrying a dripping red bundle that had moments before been our vivacious Dyllie.

It was only when we reached the vet's office and handed our bundle to the doctor that I realized the howling was coming from me. I collected myself and sat down in the waiting room, blood-covered hands laying haphazardly on my lap. The smell of warm, fresh, blood, seemingly so filled with life, wafted into my hyperventilated nostrils. The nurse approached.

"I think you should wash your hands."

As I headed toward the bathroom, the doctor emerged from the operating room. Our eyes met; he shook his head, confirming what we already knew.

"Do you want her ashes?" he asked. I shook my head. Dyllie was gone; I did not believe her essence could be preserved in charred remains. She was now, once again, part of the universe.

We paid the bill and left with an emptied, blood-stained sweatshirt. Instinctively, Joel and I put our arms around one another as we walked home. When we arrived at the corner where Dyllie had died, many of the onlookers were still there. Many wiped away tears when they saw Joel's empty hands.

Several bystanders had chased down the taxi driver, forcing him to return to the scene. He sat motionless in his car, head lowered, resting it on the steering wheel. The police had arrived.

Joel and I looked at each other. Condemnation and punishment would not bring Dyllie back. Perhaps the taxicab driver would learn a vital lesson and not run any more red lights. Perhaps Dyllie's death would save the life of a child.

Dyllie was run over twice—first, by the car's front tire, and then, a few seconds later, the back. In the moment between the two blows, she rose, undaunted, ready for her next battle.

Dyllie died on the streets of Manhattan as she lived—bold, unafraid, defiant.

After I returned to the apartment, I realized I had not exchanged a single word with the woman or her husband. As soon as I walked in the door, I jumped into the shower, citing the heat as the reason for a second shower that day. I couldn't bring myself to tell Joel what had happened. There had been so many COVID deaths that somehow watching a stranger's dog die on the streets of Manhattan did not elicit a normal reaction from me. Despite my efforts to help the woman, and even despite the memory of Dyllie, I remained strangely detached. The unfolding scene was more akin to watching a movie than watching an animal take its last breath. It also occurred to me that Dyllie's death reminded me of the homeless. In many ways, they lived as Dyllie died— bold, unafraid, defiant.

However, when I climbed into bed later that night, I started to sweat profusely, a reminder that I might not have been as unaffected by the experience as I believed. The puppy's death made me think of all the COVID victims who'd lost their lives. If losing a dog could result in such profound sorrow for its owner, how must people feel who'd lost a loved one? When will this nightmare end? I thought as I drifted off to sleep, grateful for the few hours of oblivion it promised.

August continued to bring more forward movement, coupled with backward slides, and mixed messages about the widely-rumored fears of a second wave. On August 5th, Dr. Fauci predicted that the country could overcome the virus without shutting down the economy again.

"There seems to be a misrepresentation that either you shut down completely and damage a lot of things, mental health, the economy, all kinds of things, or let it rip and do whatever you want. There's a stepwise fashion that you can open up the economy successfully." Fauci ended his message by stressing the need for all Americans to work together and practice social distancing, the wearing of face masks, and hand hygiene.

On August 7th, Governor Cuomo announced that New York schools would be allowed to reopen in September. The news was met with applause from some, concern from many, and scorn by a few naysayers who seemed content only with a continued shutdown.

Many teachers expressed concern. They would be the ones spending hours every day in classrooms with numerous students who everyone knew could contract the virus. Governor Cuomo expressed his support, but nevertheless, concluded that teachers were going to have to show up for work, or find different jobs. Cuomo left it up to the school districts to decide how to reopen safely. In the end, most chose a hybrid model of teaching in which students were in the classrooms half of the time and attending from home, online, the other half.

New York State continued to beat the odds and defy predictions. *The New York Times* reported the surprising facts—only one percent of the 30,000 COVID tests being administered each day were positive. The low incidence was in sharp contrast to other large cities. Los Angeles reported a seven percent positive daily test rate, and Miami, a staggering thirteen percent. "New York is like our South Korea now," said Dr. Thomas Tsai of the Harvard Global Health Institute.

New Yorkers' hard-earned results were rewarded by the news that gyms would be allowed to reopen on August 24th and museums the following week. Most people welcomed the announced openings, yet one question remained unanswered—when would indoor dining resume?

Joel made the morning rounds without me on Friday. When we met in the apartment that evening, he reported unusual news.

"Virtually no one was on the street today."

"Does anyone know anything?" I asked.

"I asked the Starbucks manager if she'd seen Bob. She looked at the security tape. An ambulance arrived in the middle of the night and stopped just beside the telephone booth."

"Oh no, not again. He's been in the hospital so many times already."

Joel's telephone rang. Somehow, I knew it was bad news even before I heard Joel exclaim, "Oh, God, no."

"What happened?" Joel said. He put on the speaker and placed his phone on the table between us.

"I got beat up with a golf club last night," Bob said, his voice trembling.

"Why would anyone beat you up with a golf club?" Joel asked.

"Two white men said Cathy owed them ten dollars and she was my woman so I was taking the beating for her. It makes no sense. They beat me so bad over ten dollars."

"I'm so sorry this happened to you, Bob," Joel replied. "I'll be down in twenty minutes."

Neither of us felt like finishing our dinner, so Joel left and I cleaned up. An hour later, Joel returned with details.

"Bob told me he was asleep when suddenly he felt the first blow to his back. He said all he could think about was all the Black men who'd been whipped over the last several hundred years."

"Awful."

"He said he immediately crawled into the fetal position to protect his head. The blows kept coming for ten minutes. He was covered in bandages from his back to his ankles. And they sliced open the pocket of his jeans and took the sixteen dollars he had."

"Why didn't he stay in the hospital a bit longer?" I asked.

"The hospital told him to stay, but you know Bob—he wanted to get back to the telephone booth as quickly as possible in case Cathy showed up."

"Since she's not there, couldn't he go to his mother's apartment for a few days?" I asked.

"I suggested that. He said his mother is too fragile to see him all beat up."

"Did he report it to the police?"

"No. You know he thinks the police wouldn't help him."

"Does he have any idea where Cathy is?"

"Nowhere to be found, per usual these days. Ever since she got the diagnosis of Hep-C, she's really spun out," Joel said. "I really hope she's not on crack."

"Same. I'm so worried about her. By the way, was Tony there?"

"He did show up, all arms and legs jumping around. He was horrified."

"We have to get Bob off the street before he dies."

"I'm going to write to his case worker again," Joel promised.

"And Tony's too. Please write to his case worker. It's been twenty-four years—how many years does a person have to be homeless around here?" I knew the demand for safe haven rooms was tight. But if Bob and Tony couldn't get a room then who could? "What else did Bob say?"

"He asked me if it was time to let Cathy go."

"What did you say?"

"I told him it was time to take care of himself—his ailing heart and kidney disease, not to mention the water in his legs and surrounding his lungs."

Despite Joel's conversation with Bob, the next morning Bob was doing a little better and Cathy was back in the telephone booth sitting beside him, both acting as if everything was okay.

The following week the YMCA on 47th Street—our Y—announced they had made an arrangement with a city agency to house homeless people in the two hundred rooms that had once served as inexpensive lodging for youths traveling from abroad. While I was delighted that two hundred homeless people would soon be sheltered, I also realized the impact that having a shelter in an affluent neighborhood would have on the surrounding property values. And selfishly, it occurred to me we would have to find another gym, as our pool would remain closed.

The next morning, Bob shared the good news that he'd been offered a room at our Y! Against all odds, Bob's case worker had come through with a third room. Bob was ecstatic. So were we.

"It's a real good room too," Bob said with a big smile.

"Do you have a roommate or is it a single?"

"I'm in a single room and it has a flat screen TV, small refrigerator, and air conditioning. How great is that?"

"Wonderful! How's the bed?" Joel asked.

"The mattress is at least six inches thick! Feels real good."

"Make sure you check in there once every three days," Joel warned. "There won't be a fourth room if you lose this one."

"I'll be sleeping there every night," Bob assured us. "But somehow putting us homeless people there does not seem right. It's a real nice neighborhood."

"Well, that's up to the Y to decide," Joel said. "And in any event, congratulations!"

On the way home, Joel and I had a further conversation about the situation.

"I feel bad for the apartment owners on 47th Street," he admitted.

"Me too. It's going to be practically impossible for them to sell their apartments. As if the situation with the pandemic isn't bad enough for all property owners here in the city."

"I bet there are some pretty upset people. I know it would not be my first choice to have a shelter on our street," Joel admitted.

And there it was—the ugly truth. While most people agreed, in principle, that society should help the homeless, no one wanted them in their neighborhoods. The NIMBYist movement—Not In My Back

Yard—was in full swing. If Joel and I wouldn't want a shelter on our block after getting to know so many homeless people in the previous six months, then who would be okay with it?

Not many people on the Upper West Side, apparently. The entire area was in turmoil over the use of two hotels—the Lucerne and the Hotel Belleclaire—to shelter the homeless, allegedly to stop the spread of the virus within shelters. Mayor de Blasio stepped in to the escalating debate when legal action was threatened, calling for the removal of over two hundred homeless people.

David Giffen, Executive Director of Coalition for the Homeless said, "The Mayor's decision to capitulate to the NIMBYist voices on the Upper West Side by further displacing homeless New Yorkers is a sad victory for the well-heeled and well-connected whose fear-mongering and intolerance disgrace our city. It is inhumane and just plain wrong."

The following week, de Blasio reversed his decision calling for a further review of the entire homeless problem in the city, stating, "We're going to look at the whole shelter system and the whole question of what we should or should not be doing in hotels at this point. And then we will figure out quickly what next steps to take."

The question of where to shelter the homeless was becoming a national debate, especially in urban areas. The pandemic had caused what had long been an issue that could be ignored to one that was front and center. Governor Newsom of California had devoted his entire State of the State address in February to the issue after a USC Price-USC Schwarzenegger poll showed that California voters named homelessness as the number one issue they were concerned about (23%), followed by climate change at 15% and immigration at 9%.

Despite the fight over the use of hotels on the Upper West Side to house the homeless during the pandemic, a New York News Channel 1 survey revealed that the majority of New Yorkers believed that homeless people should be housed in hotels and shelters in their *own* neighborhoods. Californians and New Yorkers were not the only citizens whose growing awareness of the latent homelessness epidemic was igniting a passionate cry for something, anything, to be done. According to a poll conducted by Data for Progress, 60% of voters said they wanted a public option for housing for all Americans.

We continued to make our rounds, even though most of our friends were now sheltered. One day we ran into Wayne, the man who'd lost his wife and children on the New Jersey turnpike. The corner where Maggie and Rick had lived for three years was now empty.

"Where is everyone?" Wayne asked.

"Everyone except Cathy and Tony are sheltered," Joel replied with a big smile.

"Well, how about that!" Wayne exclaimed. "I'd never thought the pandemic would end up helping homeless folks."

"Yeah, how about that," Joel replied.

Even though we were delighted that most of our homeless friends were now sheltered, and that everyone had finally been assigned a case worker, we knew that getting the last two of our original group into safe haven rooms was not going to be easy. While hotels were helping to improve the lives of the homeless who were already in shelters, very few of those rooms were being used to house the group of homeless people living on the streets. There seemed to be an unspoken pecking order among the homeless and those who slept on the streets were in the lowest tier.

Tony had been homeless for twenty-four years; Cathy for over twenty. Ironically, it seemed the longer a person had been homeless, the harder it was to house them. Somehow, once they dropped out of the shelter system and ended up on the streets, they fell through the figurative cracks in the sidewalk. Nevertheless, I was hopeful that a room would soon be found for Cathy because she was a woman and now physically at risk due to her Hep-C diagnosis. Tony's fate posed more of a concern.

"Please write to their case workers," I urged Joel again that night. I could have written to them myself, but at that point, they all knew Joel was not only a licensed mental health counselor but also an ordained interfaith minister. Not surprisingly, they responded better to a minister than to a lawyer.

"I'll write as soon as we finish dinner," Joel agreed.

"Thanks. Tony is not getting off the street easily. And of all of our people, he's the only one working. He deserves a room if anyone does."

■ – ■ – ■

MAGGIE WRIGHT, AUGUST 2020

After being on the streets about two years, I was finally able to obtain benefits, such as food stamps and Medicaid. I received $234 a month in food stamps, which I quickly learned was not to be spent on food. Scattered across the city are bodegas, which will exchange food stamps for cash, at a discounted price. Most places will pay sixty cents on the dollar, so my $234 was worth approximately $140. People must think that is ridiculous. The homeless are starving, and yet, they sell their food stamps? What most people do not know is that food stamps cannot be used to purchase hot, prepared foods. And since many of the homeless are not in possession of stoves, ovens and microwaves, they are not so useful.

In general, people living on the streets want to sell their food stamps. This presents a whole new set of problems. One, is finding a place that actually does it—a lot of places won't, since if they get caught they can lose their ability to accept food stamps. Another is finding someone trustworthy.

For example, one night, I went into a bodega to buy a soda and a bag of chips. When I checked my receipt, the man had charged me $130. If I had not noticed, I would have lost the money.

As a last ditch effort, if you cannot find a place that will exchange them, you can buy things to sell to the bodegas, such as Red Bulls, Ensures, and ice cream. The bodegas pay $1 per drink or ice cream bar. That is another way to "cash in your stamps."

William was a pro at exchanging food stamps, and, before he was sheltered, he searched the city for the best deal. He found it in Brooklyn—a tiny bodega in a horrible neighborhood that paid ninety cents on the dollar. Once we discovered that place, I told all my homeless friends about it.

While homelessness in New York City introduced me to the selling of food stamps, I was no stranger to selling "prized possessions" for money. When I was still in New Jersey, I convinced my doctor to prescribe Adderall and Xanax. After I became homeless, I would pick up my meds, and Rick and I would head to Atlantic Avenue and sit on the steps outside the library and sell the pills. $5 for Adderall, $7 for Xanax. That was good money for Atlantic City, considering you couldn't earn more than $10 a day there panhandling.

Unfortunately, that windfall ended when Rick slipped some crack into a blunt he gave me, and I tested positive for cocaine in my monthly drug test. I was smart enough to take one pill from each prescription before the test so my urine would show traces of the medications but not smart enough to know that Rick would slip crack into my blunt.

After that, I had to sell my things. First to go was my Pandora bracelet. That one hurt the most. It had taken years to acquire those charms. Each one was special and had a story behind it—the menorah, the pig, the Jets logo. It was priceless to me. In the end, Rick sold it for $12. Next on the auction block was my violet Coach bag—the one my friend had rigged the raffle at her daughter's fundraiser to ensure I won. The retail value was $800. Homeless woman selling it on the corner value? $10.

CHAPTER 14

Shattered Hopes and Dreams

———■———

In the beginning of September, restaurant owners filed a class action lawsuit against both city and state officials, alleging that irreparable harm had been caused to their businesses as a result of the shutdowns. The complaint demanded two billion dollars in damages. Unfortunately, Jan was too sick by this point to join the fight. She'd been in and out of the hospital more than a dozen times, and Richard Kelley, my former editor, had also been hospitalized and diagnosed with cancer. As unbelievable as it seemed, I became afraid they both might die.

Jan's health was the most precarious. After a series of medical tests, her doctor finally diagnosed that her liver was not functioning properly. She confessed to having consumed excessive amounts of alcohol during the previous six months. Jan needed a transplant, and she needed it quickly.

When she was told that she had been moved up on the transplant list and was able to leave the hospital for a few days, she rallied. I was finally able to visit her on the Sunday before Labor Day. When I walked into her living room, Jan was lying on the couch in a semi-fetal position, a blanket covering her frail body, despite the heat. Her two daughters were by her side. Her husband, Ramiro, was in the kitchen making lunch.

Jan was unrecognizable. Once weighing over two hundred pounds even after gastro bypass surgery, she now had to be less than half that. Her mouth and eyes were sunken in, her face was wrinkled and sagging, aging her well beyond her fifty-six years. I did my best to hide my shock.

"You don't look so bad for someone who's been in the hospital for the last three months," I said in an effort to reassure her.

She knew it wasn't true, yet smiled anyway. I sat beside her, and we hugged. We stayed in that embrace for several minutes. She sat more upright during our visit, especially after I was able to get her to drink a little bit of a banana and peanut butter smoothie. We spoke of our early days together when she was our nanny. We laughed remembering some of the funny things the kids had done over the years.

I could tell that she needed to rest, so I kept the visit short, promising to return the following weekend. Despite my assurances, I had a gut feeling that I would never see her again.

"I love you," I said as I gave her one last hug before leaving.

"I love you too," she replied as she closed her eyes and drifted off to sleep.

The next morning she was hospitalized for the tenth time in less than a few months.

Unable to help either Jan or Richard, Joel and I shifted our attention to those we could, and our top priority was focusing on finding shelter for the last two people in our group, Cathy and Tony.

"It was sixty-two degrees last night. The cold weather is coming and I just know I'm going to be stuck out here another winter," Tony complained.

"Tony, when you are afraid, just say *thank you universe for helping me get a room*. How would that feel?" Joel asked. Tony was silent but nodded in agreement. "And please, let the Greenwich House know you've been trying to get in contact with your case worker," Joel urged.

"My case worker still isn't coming into the city because of the virus," Tony replied.

"Talk to her on the phone then," Joel suggested.

That night, Joel wrote another impassioned email begging for assistance for Tony.

The next day Bob was doing better. Cathy had disappeared again. Bob did not know where she was. Suddenly, Tony showed up, his arms and legs flailing in all directions, per usual. It was actually an endearing quality. Tony always emanated the enthusiasm of a young child at a birthday party.

"I just came from my methadone program, and I spoke to my counselor on the computer while I was there. Oh boy, if all the computers go down, we're gonna have some problems."

"Hmm, maybe we should all think about what that might be like," Joel said, and laughed.

"I still haven't heard from my case worker. Maybe I should just have taken that room in Brooklyn."

"There was no way for you to do that, Tony. You don't make money at your job and you couldn't afford the transportation costs," Joel said, attempting to assuage his guilt.

"Yeah, that's true, but I can jump the turnstiles if I need to. All this time and no one has come out here looking for me again. I'm going to be out here another winter—I just know it."

"Don't worry, Tony. You're going to get a room. Let's try calling your case worker right now," Joel suggested. Joel dialed the number and handed the phone to Tony, who in turn handed it back to Joel.

"No answer and her voice mailbox is full," he said. Suddenly, Bob stood up and pointed to a vehicle pulling up in the curb lane.

"Look, the car is here!" Two women had arrived! One woman stayed behind the wheel while the other approached Tony.

"Who are you?" she asked Joel.

"Who am I? I'm the guy who's been out here every day during the pandemic. Who are you?"

"I'm Janet, Tony's case worker."

"Great!" said Joel. "This man has been homeless for twenty-four years. I sure hope you can find a room for him soon."

Janet ignored Joel's question and asked Tony to follow her to the car to fill out some paperwork. Ten minutes later, Tony got out of the car with a big smile on his face.

"She's coming back on Friday at one o'clock to take me to my room!" he exclaimed, with tears running down his cheeks.

"Wonderful!" Joel exclaimed, embracing Tony in a bear hug.

Later that afternoon, our joy over Tony's promised room vanished when Jan's daughter called. "Mom's been moved to intensive care."

"What are the doctors telling you?"

"Not much."

"Oh my God, I'm so sorry. I'm praying for her and all of you."

On Friday morning, Tony was at the agreed upon corner by ten o'clock, already pacing in anticipation of Janet's arrival later that afternoon. By 1:15 p.m., with no transportation van in sight, Tony started getting even more nervous. Nevertheless, he continued to wait. No one showed up, and Tony slept on the street again that night.

The following Monday, Janet's supervisor showed up at the telephone booths, made some excuses about what had gone wrong on Friday, and told Tony that Janet would be there on Thursday at one o'clock to take him to his new room. Tony was optimistic again. So were we.

Our optimism turned to sorrow that afternoon, when Jan's daughter called to tell us that Jan's heart had stopped. She was on life support. "If you want to say goodbye, you should do it now. She won't be able to respond, but I will hold the phone to her ear."

"Okay, thanks," I said. As I waited for the phone to be placed next to Jan's ear, I wondered what I would say. I knew it would be the last words I spoke to her.

"Go ahead," her daughter said. "I have the phone to her ear."

I thought about the last words my mother said to me. "Hi, Jan. I just want you to remember one thing. I love you. I love you. I love you." There was nothing left to say.

Jan's mother and younger brother were on the first plane out of Iowa on Tuesday morning. I wondered how they would quarantine once they arrived. Iowa was a new "hot spot." Maybe an exception could be made for family members who were travelling to attend a funeral?

Jan was still alive when their plane landed at LaGuardia airport that afternoon. By the time they got to the hospital in the Bronx, however, Jan had died.

Jan and I had been many things for one another over our thirty-three years of friendship. First, we were employee and employer, then business partners, often fighting over this or that challenge in the restaurant. She had been a second mother to my children, and I was an aunt to hers. Through it all, we were best friends.

On Thursday, I rearranged my work schedule so that I could be at the telephone booths by noon to send off Tony. Coincidentally, Cathy's case worker had made an appointment with her to do a psycho-social evaluation the same day. It was one of the last steps before a safe haven room was assigned, so we were cautiously optimistic Cathy would soon be sheltered.

I was a block away when I saw the unfolding scene. Bob was mad at Tony over who-knew-what and was verbally and physically accosting him. Bob's mobility had greatly improved at that point. Nevertheless, what I witnessed was more akin to a linebacker running down a football field than an old man who could barely hobble to McDonald's to use the bathroom. Then I saw Joel jump in between Bob's 240 pound frame and Tony's 150 pound one.

"Good grief—what is going on?" I yelled as I arrived. Cathy was sitting in her phone booth, seemingly nonplussed. "Cathy, what happened?" I repeated.

"Bob's all hot," she replied, stating the obvious.

"Over what?" Cathy, in typical Cathy style, just shrugged her shoulders. I headed to the corner and entered the fray.

"What's going on, guys?" I asked.

"Tony has no gratitude," Bob said.

"No gratitude about what?"

"No gratitude about nothing, no time," Bob repeated.

Joel jumped into the conversation to try to explain what Bob meant. "Bob wants the hair clippers I just gave Tony. Come on, Tony. We have to leave now."

"He can't leave," I said. "They are coming to take him to his room soon. Just go around the corner and wait over there."

Tony, who was now crying, skedaddled, and I took Bob's arm and gently led him back to his chair at the phone booth. He was huffing and puffing and mumbling, "Tony's got no gratitude. That man never say no to nothing."

"What's the big deal?" I asked and pulled out my iPhone to open my Amazon account and quickly found the exact set that Joel had just given Tony. "You want one too?" I asked. "This is supposed to be a day of joy for Tony, Bob. You have your room at the Y, but Tony is still sleeping on the streets."

At the sound of my offer to buy a hair clipper, Cathy perked up. "Can I see it?" she asked.

"Here, is this what you want?" I asked, handing her the phone.

"Oh, Bob, look," she exclaimed like a young girl opening presents on Christmas morning. "This is what Tony got."

Bob smiled. I clicked the *BUY* button. "Okay, now you have one too, Bob," I said. "It's arriving next week."

"Much appreciated," Bob replied with a self-satisfied smirk.

Suddenly, Cathy's case worker appeared, and I thought things were turning around for the better.

"Hello," I said, extending my right hand to shake hers. "I'm Traci. Thank you so much for helping Cathy. She's been homeless for over twenty years." Cathy's case worker nodded but declined to shake my hand. In my excitement, I'd momentarily forgotten we were living in the age of COVID.

"I'm going to take her for some lunch and fill out the paperwork," she said.

"Great, thanks so much." I embraced Cathy and whispered into her ear. "Everything is going to be alright." Cathy cried, then smiled, then cried some more.

Cathy's case worker put her arm around Cathy as they walked away. *Thank God. At least she is willing to touch Cathy.*

Once Cathy was out of sight, I turned my attention back to Bob who was sitting in the telephone booth with his head lowered. I was torn between the opposing desires to comfort and to kick him.

"I'm going to hang out with Joel and Tony to wait for the transportation van."

"Don't let him fool you with those crocodile tears," Bob replied, looking up.

"Cut it out, Bob. You've drained enough positive energy out of this corner today."

Bob lowered his head again and a tear rolled down his cheek. I walked away, unwilling to further reward his inappropriate behavior. I was mad at myself for buying the hair clippers to placate him, but it was Tony's moment, and I didn't want it spoiled.

I found Tony huddled in a fetal position with Joel bent down comforting him. It was now 1:30 p.m., and the transportation van had not yet arrived.

"It's going to be okay," Joel assured him. "Maggie is on her way too."

Suddenly, Maggie appeared as she had promised. When she realized what was happening, she became pissed. "They've been promising him a room for two weeks," she said.

Finally, Janet arrived.

"Great, you're here," I said. "Tony, Janet is here to take you to your room." Janet looked worried and shook her head.

"You don't have a room for him?" I asked.

Janet didn't answer.

"I have to speak with Tony," she said. Tony stood up and walked away with Janet.

"Wait, I'm coming with you," Joel said. "I'm his advocate and he has given permission for me to be included in any conversation."

"I can't talk to you," Janet replied, shaking her head.

"What do you mean, you can't talk to me? Tony, tell her you give permission."

"Yes, this is my advocate," Tony confirmed.

"I can't talk to you," Janet repeated.

"Tony just gave you permission," Joel said, arms spread wide in disbelief. Tony started to cry again and Janet backed away.

"I'm calling my case worker," Maggie said. As soon as Lina answered the phone Maggie let loose. "This is a disaster here. Janet does not have a room for Tony," she screamed into the phone. Janet glanced over at Maggie.

"You told this man twice that you had a room for him," Joel said.

"I had a room for him last week at The Andrews. He turned it down," Janet replied.

"That's a lie," Tony said. "I ain't turned down no room here in Manhattan. I'll take any room you got where I can walk to work."

"You can't talk to me that way," Janet said, and walked away.

William appeared, and Maggie ran over to tell him what had happened. We were all heartbroken for Tony. There were few things more devastating for a homeless person than being promised a room only to lose it at the last minute.

The next morning, a man identifying himself as a supervisor called my cell phone. It was clear that there was confusion about what had gone wrong with Tony's room. After a cordial thirty minute conversation, we agreed that something had to be done.

"Regardless of who said what to whom, or who did what to whom, Tony has been homeless for twenty-four years," I explained. "Surely our society can do better than that for its homeless citizens. Surely, we must do better than that," I said.

"We're working on it around the clock," the supervisor promised.

"Great, make it happen then." I pleaded, practically begging.

The Jewish New Year arrived on September 18th and brought with it an abundance of riches. It was Maggie's birthday weekend and she was doing very well. She diligently made her rounds checking on our group every day, including her birthday.

"I have good news," she said, when she called me in the late afternoon. "There is one room left at The Travelers, and Lina is trying to get it for Tony."

"OMG, that is just great! We need to find him to let him know."

"I'll find him," Maggie promised.

"Okay, great. Please keep me posted. Joel and I are heading up to Mahopac tomorrow morning to visit with Jan's family. Her funeral is Monday, so I won't be back to the city until Tuesday."

"Okay, Tray, I'm so sorry again about Jan. I'll keep you posted about Tony."

Despite having spent the whole day looking for him, Maggie could not find Tony, so I decided to call the bodega the next morning as we drove up to Mahopac.

"Hello, may I please speak with Tony?"

"Who?" An unidentified man answered the phone with a clear "what do you want" tone.

"Tony. He works as a janitor in your bodega. He's Hispanic, mid-fifties. Small and skinny."

"There is no one working here by that name or description."

Click.

"I think they're pretending Tony does not work there because they don't pay him."

"Right, they may think you're someone from the Labor Department," Joel agreed.

"I'm going to try again."

"Tell them who you are as soon as they answer," Joel suggested.

"Hello, I just called. My name is Traci Rosow. I'm a friend of Tony's. He's been homeless for twenty-four years, and we have a room for him. Please, I need to find him." There was a moment of silence.

"What's your phone number?" the man asked. I gave it to him, thanked him profusely, and hung up.

Thirty minutes later, we arrived in Mahopac. I had reserved a swim lane at Club Fit so I gave my phone to Joel in case Tony called while I was in the water and couldn't answer it.

"If Tony calls, tell him to call Maggie immediately." Thirty minutes later, I was back in the car and before I could ask if Tony had called, Joel shouted, "He called!"

"Yay! Did you tell him to call Maggie?"

"I did indeed."

"Okay, great. Now we wait."

While Maggie was helping Tony, we spent Friday afternoon with Jan's husband, daughters, mother, and brother. Despite Jan's physical absence, I was unable to believe she had really died. At Christmas, she'd been her usual vibrant and busy self. Could stress really have caused an otherwise seemingly healthy person to die so quickly?

The sadness of the afternoon lifted in the evening, when Maggie sent a picture of Tony holding up the keys to his new safe haven room. It had been a long time since I'd seen an expression as triumphant as Tony's in that picture.

I showed the picture to Joel. "Happy New Year!" he shouted.

Later that evening, I lay in bed reading and feeling a glow from the knowledge that Tony would be sleeping in a bed that night when a flashing news bubble on my iPhone captured my attention. *Ruth Bader Ginsburg, dead at age eighty-seven.*

And just like that, my mood went from joyous to morose. RBG had fought so hard for her life, her fellow gender, her country. I wondered if she'd somehow *chosen* the Jewish New Year as the day to start the next leg of her journey.

Saturday morning, Maggie called in a panic. William had disappeared.

"This is not like William, Tray. He's either been arrested or is in the hospital."

"Where were you when you last saw him?"

"We were sitting on a park bench downtown. He said he needed to go to the store and would be right back."

"Why didn't you go with him?"

"I thought he was going to buy a card or some flowers for my birthday."

"You just waited on the park bench all night?"

"No, we always agreed that if we got separated, we'd meet back at his apartment. So I went to Brooklyn and waited on the stoop all night. He never showed up."

"Why didn't you go inside?"

"I didn't have my key."

"Why didn't you call him?"

"He lost his phone yesterday."

"Where are you now?"

"I just got to The Travelers."

"Good, take a hot shower and try to get some sleep. Call me when you wake up."

Four hours later, Maggie called in a heightened panic. Still no word from William. She left The Travelers intent on tracking him down. Thirty minutes later, she called again.

"He's alive," she said. "But I'm going to kill him when I get there."

As it turned out, William had indeed gone to the store to buy some flowers. Unfamiliar with the downtown area, he'd gotten lost and could not find the park bench where Maggie was waiting. He returned home, per their agreement. While she sat on the front stoop, he was upstairs pacing in his room, waiting for her return, unaware that she did not have her key. And of course, like the rest of us, he did not know Maggie's phone number by heart, having always pulled it up in his contacts on the few occasions he needed to call her. That method was of no use because William had lost his phone.

The next morning, William set out to find her and ran into Tony who still had Maggie's phone number from the day before.

"Talk about your good deed being returned to you," I said to Maggie. "Tony had your number because you were trying to get a room for him, so he was able to give your number to William."

"Yeah, it's crazy," she said. "I've never had a mitzvah returned so quickly."

After Jan's funeral on Monday morning, we went back to her house and looked at old photos—Jan with our children when they were young, Jan with her daughters, and Jan with me. It had been a long weekend of saying goodbye. Friday afternoon visit with family, wake on Sunday, and funeral on Monday. *How did it come to this?* I asked myself over and over. Jan, one of the most vivacious women I'd ever known, now gone.

On Tuesday afternoon, we saw Maggie.

"I have good news!" she shouted as she spotted us walking down Park Avenue.

"And?" Joel replied.

"I'm going to see the kids next week!" Joel and I exchanged glances. I knew he was as skeptical as I was about Maggie's claim. Nevertheless, I hoped she would visit. "There's more good news," she continued. "Rick has been reunited with his children and is having lunch with his mother and older son next week. And his second wife has agreed to allow him to assist in the homeschooling of his younger son."

"How many sons does he have?" Joel asked. I realized we never knew exactly how many children Rick had.

"He has two kids by his first wife and one son by his second wife. She's agreed to his offer to help their son, probably because she has seven other children under the age of eight!" Maggie said.

"Rick has seven children?"

"No, she does. She has six other children including three sets of twins, all with different fathers," Maggie explained.

"I guess she does need some help then," Joel quipped.

On Thursday night, Maggie called bubbling with excitement.

"Tray, they just came for Cathy! She got a safe haven room at the Y, one floor above Bob!"

"Oh, wow, that is just the best news. They always wanted to stay together."

I went to bed that night with a weight off my shoulders. All of our homeless friends were sheltered. The city had reopened. The virus was on the wane.

No one yet knew that Omicron was coming.

■ – ■ – ■

MAGGIE WRIGHT, SEPTEMBER 2020

When you live on the streets, you meet lots of different people. Everyone has a story to tell, and there are always some people you like more than others. For me, Tony was one of my favorite homeless friends. I had known him for years. He was tiny, virtually my size, and thus, I was not afraid of him. He was an alcoholic, but a kind one. Like clockwork, I would find him outside the liquor store in the morning, waiting for it to open. The rest of his day consisted of hunting for bottles and cans to cash in to buy more booze. He worked hard for his money, and he never bothered anyone or stole. As I said, he was a good one.

He was also a responsible one. He was the only homeless person I knew who owned a storage unit, a pretty big deal for a homeless person. Not only did it ensure his things would not be stolen, on particularly cold or rainy nights, Tony could grab a couple of hours of sleep there. He never divulged where his storage unit was, and I respected him for that.

I was thrilled when I found out he was finally getting a room. Getting a room is a very big deal to a homeless person. It is also a terrifying experience, as most homeless people thrive on routine, and any change is frightening. It is very easy to get discouraged, lose hope, and lose out on a room because of red tape. That's one of the reasons I took it personally when each of my homeless friends obtained housing, and I always tried to be there to see them off and root them on for the next stage.

Tony was no exception. When Traci and Joel told me he had finally obtained housing, I was thrilled and would not have missed seeing him be picked up on his big day. As soon as I arrived at the designated spot, however, I knew something was wrong. Tony was hysterical, Bob was screaming, and things seemed to be generally amiss.

I was used to Bob being obnoxious. While I appreciated him as a person, he irritated me because he did not like to see good things happen to other people. He became jealous and often times ruined happy moments for others.

When Tony's caseworker finally showed up, she informed Tony that she did not have a room for him. That was more than I could take. I knew how this worked. This problem could very well scare Tony off from seeking help ever again, and he'd been homeless for almost twenty-five years. No one likes to be disappointed, and to a homeless person, being told you are going to sleep in a warm bed only to be told you won't be, can be a breaking point.

I went ballistic. I called my caseworker, Lina, and told her what was going on. I was lucky. My caseworker was one of the best. Lina promised she would see what she could do. I called Tony over to where I was standing and spoke to him calmly. I asked him to not give up. He was crying and obviously crestfallen.

True to her word, Lina came through and was able to get Tony the last available room at The Travelers. It took two days to find him, but when he had that key in his hand, and that smile across his face, I felt warm and fuzzy inside. I snapped a picture to send to Traci. It was Rosh Hashanah. I took this to be a sign that it was a new year and only wonderful things were coming!

CHAPTER 15

Descending Darkness

■

Fall officially arrived and with it came noticeably busier streets. Many *For Rent* signs remained on boarded-up store fronts, but other businesses were starting to reopen. On September 30th, just in time to address the cooler night temperatures, New York City restaurants were finally allowed to offer indoor dining, at twenty-five percent capacity.

In October, Henry, the older man who was one of the first of our friends to obtain shelter back in June, finally reappeared. We were out making our morning rounds when Joel spotted him on the east side of Park Avenue.

"Look!" he shouted, pointing across the street. "That's Henry!" We both started screaming his name, and Henry came bounding across six lanes of traffic without looking in either direction.

"Where have you been?" Joel asked, giving him a bear hug.

"Upstate."

"What do you mean, upstate?" Joel asked.

"Back in prison for missing my parole meeting. Truth be told, I've skipped the last four years of meetings."

"How did you get away with that?" Joel asked.

"It's hard to find a homeless person on the streets."

"Have you called your case worker yet?" I asked, turning our attention away from the celebration at Henry's return and back to the reality that he was, once again, homeless."

"Not yet," Henry confessed.

Joel handed Henry his cell phone. "Maybe you should call her now?' At this point, we had all of our homeless friends' case worker's names, email addresses and cell phone numbers in our contacts. Henry's case worker answered, and he explained where he had been and why. She promised to find him another safe haven room soon. Right, I thought. My skepticism, fortunately, proved ill-founded. The following week, Henry was safely sheltered once again.

"By the way, how did your parole officer find you after four years?" Joel asked.

"From the shelter system. Once I was registered as sheltered, they knew where I was sleeping."

"Wow, I never thought about that," Joel confessed. "I guess that's the downside of finally getting off the streets."

"Yeah, and it only took them a week to come get me," Henry said.

"We're on our way to see Bob and Cathy," Joel said. "Come with us."

The three of us walked down Park Avenue to the telephone booths and found Bob, Cathy and Tony. Everyone was ecstatic to see Henry again. No one knew where he had been since he'd disappeared.

"Let's take a picture," I urged them. First, the three men embraced, and I took pictures as I shouted, "The boys are back in town!" Pedestrians gave me questioning and worried looks as they quickly passed by the spectacle.

The October days were glorious, but the cold weather was already returning to the city and the nights were chilly. Joel decided to use the last of the donation money to buy everyone a winter coat. As the packages arrived, the piles of coats on our couch grew tall, creating a kaleidoscope of colors in our living room.

"How are we going to decide who gets which coat?" Joel asked.

"Well, this pink one is obviously for Maggie," I said. "Why don't we just let everyone else pick for themselves?"

"What about Cathy?"

"She will want a man's coat, so let her pick too," I replied. "And then, we're done. They all have rooms, new clothes, new shoes, and winter coats. It's time to let go. We've done everything we can for them."

"Right, right," Joel replied, distracted, as he looked at his iPad.

"Right, you agree?" I probed. "Everyone is sheltered. Can we get back to our lives now?"

"What do you think about these winter hats?" he asked, handing me his iPad.

November ushered in noticeably cooler temperatures, and with it, the much-awaited election. Even after it was over, after the votes were counted and recounted, after President-elect Biden was certified as the winner, the country did not have closure. But on Monday morning, November 9th, when Pfizer announced its COVID vaccine was 90% effective, nothing else seemed to matter for a while.

Thanksgiving approached, and New Yorkers prepared to limit, or even cancel, gatherings. We got up early and made bags full of turkey sandwiches and set out. We were grateful that not a single one of our friends was on the street that morning except Kyle, who, as usual, rain or shine, holiday or not, had to earn enough money to buy the heroin he needed to keep from going into withdrawal. My heart sank when he saw us and broke out running towards us with opened arms.

I realized that even once sheltered, most of our friends were still panhandling to collect enough money to support their addictions, be it alcohol, drugs, or both.

After we'd finished handing out sandwiches, Maggie and I went to the grocery store and purchased the essentials for a Thanksgiving meal. As she prepared her dinner later that afternoon, she sent pictures of her bounty. It was clear Maggie was a good cook. It was the first Thanksgiving she'd enjoyed in four years, and William's first in over twenty.

The previous year, we'd crammed twenty family members into our apartment—this year it was just us and the kids. We played a game. Everyone shared one thing they were grateful for that the pandemic had brought about for our family. We went around in a circle until no one could think of anything else to add to the list. When we were done, there were more than twenty items of gratitude. Looking at that list, I realized the many ways in which gratitude manifests. It's often subtle, but no less meaningful.

The see-saw so characteristic of 2020 tipped in the positive direction when on Friday, December 11th, the FDA announced it had granted emergency-use approval to the Pfizer vaccine. By Saturday, the first doses were being prepared for shipment to hospitals and nursing homes. On Monday, we watched the news as the first emergency care nurse in New York was vaccinated on Long Island.

After the Electoral College confirmed Joe Biden's win, the country moved one step closer to a peaceful transition of power. Then, the first winter snowstorm approached, and New Yorkers prepared for the worst. On December 15th more snow fell in the city than in the entire previous winter. As when New Yorkers had pitched in to clean up litter when the trash cans were removed in the summer, they now emerged from their homes to shovel the sidewalks.

To most people's disappointment, indoor dining was prohibited once again. The few remaining restaurants pushed forward with outdoor dining using a plethora of heat lamps. Peter and I bought thermal underwear, bundled up, and continued eating our lunches outside. For the most part, it was okay. We weren't warm, but we managed.

As Christmas approached and we again planned to celebrate without our extended families, I realized that all any of us could do was play our own part—wearing our masks, social distancing, washing our hands, helping to support the struggling businesses in our neighborhoods. Little bits of help from a lot of people added up to make a difference to those who were struggling.

This was also a way to honor the 350,000 Americans who had already lost their lives to the virus and the many hundreds of thousands more predicted to succumb to it before the worst was over. It seemed the least we could do for the families who would miss seeing their loved ones around the dinner table, not just that Christmas, but forever.

On January 3rd, we returned to Turks to finish the vacation that had abruptly ended the year before. The trip was an act of overcoming obstacles, as we obtained the necessary negative coronavirus tests for ourselves and the exit and entry permits needed to travel with the dogs. The only easy part of the trip was the airport and plane because both were empty. Very few people were willing to travel at that point. Chad offered to make rounds on our behalf and keep us posted about our homeless friends' well-being and whereabouts while we were gone.

If possible, the suffering we witnessed upon our arrival in Turks felt even more acute than what we had left behind in New York. With tourism accounting for over eighty percent of the Turks' economy, thousands of residents had been out of work for ten months. The locals were food insecure.

Adding to the widespread suffering, on January 6th the world watched as a large number of people stormed the Capitol. As the virus raged out of control across the country and Arizona became the latest "hot spot," over four thousand more Americans had lost their lives by nightfall. It was the highest daily death toll to date from the virus. Everyone prayed it was the peak. It wasn't.

Even in Turks, even in paradise, the locals watched their televisions in disbelief. I realized that despite the often unflattering comments made about the United States, many people still see the country as their protector. That thin layer of comfort seemed to be stripping away. I heard people referring to our country as the "new Nicaragua."

As I went to sleep that night amidst the cries for Vice President Pence's support of the 25th Amendment and House Speaker Nancy

Pelosi's promise to begin a second impeachment, I reflected on just how far down our country had fallen in the last few years. I wondered if it really had to be this way.

The following week, Turks received its first supply of vaccine from the UK. Amazingly, the health care workers were willing, if not eager, to jab anyone who rolled up their sleeve.

"I can't believe it," I said to Joel. "I got an appointment for us this afternoon to get our shots."

"You're kidding?"

"Nope, and the woman said they had the Pfizer vaccine."

We ended up getting our shots in what appeared to be a third-world pharmacy. In normal times, I don't think I would have gone to that pharmacy for any reason. But these were not normal times. As I snaked my way to the front of the line, I couldn't believe our good luck.

Another piece of good luck befell us while we were in Turks when I met a woman, Anne Stembler, the CEO of Hand in Hand of Glynn, a new not-for-profit agency dedicated to building tiny homes for homeless adults in Georgia. When she told me her plan, I knew this was the best path forward to helping homeless people.

Her project was inspiring, if not daunting, by any standards. She and her colleague, Linda Heagy, treasurer of Hand in Hand of Glynn, had purchased through community donations an under-utilized church and the surrounding land in Brunswick, a city just a few miles from their affluent neighborhood on Sea Island. In contrast to the multi-million dollar homes on the ocean, Brunswick is one of a handful of cities in the state of Georgia where half of the households earn less than $25,000 a year. Upwards of sixty percent of the city residents live below the poverty line.

"I just couldn't drive over that bridge one more time and not try to do something to help," Anne told me, referring to the bridge that connected Sea Island to the rest of the state.

"Your concept is certainly interesting and inspiring to say the least," I said. "I know a little bit about homelessness myself. Joel and I spent the last year trying to help the homeless people in our New York City neighborhood."

Anne had read that government funding to support a homeless person cost the state of Georgia $40,000, whereas a person, once sheltered and with consistent social services, cost approximately $13,000 a year. I recalled reading a report from Texas that estimated the state spent $90,000 a year on each of its non-sheltered residents. For us, however, the issue of shelter was not a financial one. We'd witnessed the positive transformation in all of our friends once they had a roof over their heads. We weren't naïve, though—we knew how hard it would be for each of them to keep their assigned rooms.

"If even half of them hold on to their place, I'll be happy," I said.

"Yeah, we have to be realistic. But I'm hoping for a seventy percent retention rate," Joel replied.

Anne and Linda planned to renovate the church and turn it into a community center that would be surrounded by sixty tiny homes for single adults. A variety of support services would be offered to her soon-to-be residents—everything from counseling to medical services, to assistance in finding and keeping a job.

"One of the requirements for housing will be community service on the property in lieu of a requirement for a job," Anne announced with conviction. "We're hoping that employment will eventually come later."

I couldn't bring myself to tell Anne what we'd learned about the issue of work. For reasons I still did not fully understand, the homeless people we knew seemed incapable of getting, much less holding down, a job. Panhandling was their profession, and by all accounts, they did seem to manage to put in a full day at the "office" doing that. The only exception we found was Tony, who somehow kept his non-paying janitor job at the bodega. I hoped Anne's residents would be able to fulfill the community service requirement.

After hearing about Anne's project, I decided to donate the proceeds from this book to Hand in Hand of Glynn. I was not expecting the proceeds to be significant, but we'd learned that even small amounts of money can be useful. Of course, I hoped for more but was realistic. After publishing two prior books, I knew about book royalties.

We returned to New York City in March and took up where we left off. It soon became clear just how difficult it would be for our friends to fully reintegrate into society, despite being sheltered. We found Kyle on the street corner looking unshaven and disheveled.

"What's going on?" I asked.

"I lost my room at The Andrews."

"What happened?"

"I ran into an old friend and went on a binge. Forgot to sign in for three days," he admitted.

My heart sank. "What do you need?" I asked, remembering Karen's advice to just keep showing up, regardless of what they do.

"I could really use some new shoes," he admitted, holding up his left foot. His tennis shoes were shot.

"Size 12, right?" I asked, hiding my disappointment.

"Maybe 12 and a half, if they have that size."

"I'll bring them to you as soon as they arrive. Try to stay around here, so I can find you."

"I'm sleeping in the vestibule next to the bank on 39th," he said. "I won't be far away."

Bob and Cathy were distraught—the city had removed their telephone booths. No one knew why, except for the fact that they'd been out of use for years.

"It's okay," Joel said in an effort to reassure Bob. "You're both sheltered at the Y now."

"That booth was my home for the last ten years," Bob said, wiping away a tear.

Despite her announcement before Christmas, Maggie still had not seen her children. She never told me why. Of further concern was that she'd been offered a part-time job as a barista at Starbucks but was unable to complete the required training. She just wasn't capable of meeting the demands of having to be someplace by a certain time and remain there for a certain number of hours. I did my best to hide my disappointment but felt compelled to point out the obvious.

"You need to get some type of job or you will be dependent on welfare for the rest of your life."

"I know, Tray. And I am getting ready. I just can't do it yet."

Having learned that her parents were moving back to New York in June, she decided to take the test to get her driver's permit reinstated so she could help her mother shuttle her father, who had been diagnosed with Alzheimer's, to his numerous appointments. Maggie registered to take the learner's permit written test three times. Three times she missed her appointment.

"What's going on?" I finally asked. "Are you afraid of getting your permit back because you don't think you can come through for your mother?" Maggie lowered her head and cried. Her confidence was literally beaten out of her in the three years she had lived on the street. She would finally pass the test in September.

My own personal struggles continued when I received a phone call from my editor's brother. Richard Kelley had died the day before. His brother had found Richard face-down on the floor of his apartment. Richard had been living with Paul since his cancer diagnosis. It appeared as though Richard had taken a shower and was returning to his bedroom when he took his last breath. Richard was sixty-seven. The cause of his death indicated on his death certificate was a heart attack. Richard had no previous heart issues.

The following month, Kyle disappeared. I roamed the neighborhood looking for him and asking every homeless person I saw if they'd seen him.

"Do you know where Bear is?" I asked, using his street name. Almost every homeless person we'd met had two names—their given name and a street one. In addition to Kyle's street name, some others were Wheels, Shorty, TT, Nitty, Twin, Diaz and Moose.

No one had seen Kyle. I texted his case worker, Karen, and she said she'd run into him up at Columbus Circle. "Near the Signature Bank on the circle."

"What was he doing up there?"

"He said he moved."

"Oh, no."

"He'll be back. I can guarantee it, Traci. He knows you and Joel live in Murray Hill. He'll come back."

"I'm going up to Columbus Circle to look for him."

"If Kyle wants to be found, he'll be back. Just wait for him to return."

Despite Karen's good advice, the next morning I went uptown and spent the day canvassing the streets for Kyle. All I was left with that evening was a pair of swollen feet.

William had started drinking heavily again and was arrested three times for shoplifting. Maggie was beside herself. "William is such a great guy when he's sober. But when he drinks he turns into a jerk."

"Can't you make him get his monthly shot?"

"I can try, Tray, but even that shot is not a guarantee he won't drink."

"I thought he threw up whenever he drinks?"

"Yeah, but towards the end of the thirty days he can drink right through it. All it takes is one bad night. One old friend. One golden opportunity. And months of progress are wiped out."

"Does your case worker have any advice?"

"Oh, I thought I told you. She quit to go back to graduate school."

"Good for Lina, but not so good for you. She is the best of the best."

"You're right about that," Maggie agreed. "I don't even know who my new case worker is."

"I'm so sorry about William. As you know, I placed my cousin into one of the best treatment centers in Florida. He was there for six months. When he came out, he stayed clean for eight months. Then he took a trip to Virginia and ran into some of his old buddies. He started drinking again and was dead before Christmas."

"Yep. The vicious cycle," Maggie said.

Despite the setbacks, to our relief, everyone except Kyle was still sheltered. Bob and Cathy were at the Y. Tony and Mark still had their rooms at The Travelers. And Rick and Henry had both managed to hang on to their rooms at the Andrews.

The inevitable was approaching, however—the city was now talking about moving the homeless out of the hotels and back into shelters. This change would include places like the Y. Additionally, the rent moratorium was set to expire at the end of July, and such an event would undoubtedly leave more people homeless.

"This situation is getting worse by the day," Joel said. "I haven't even been able to get any case workers assigned to the new people in the neighborhood." At this point, we'd started helping another group of homeless men—Aubrey, Rolando, Timmy, Isaac, Bill, Harlan, and Steve, to name a few.

"I know. Thank goodness everyone in our original group, except Kyle, is off the street. If we thought things were bad during the pandemic, they seem even worse now. I'm worried about what will happen to Bob and Cathy when the Y reverts back to being a hostel."

"I agree. I have no idea why de Blasio is intent on doing this now," Joel said.

"Me neither. His announcement just said that he was going to remove all the homeless from the hotels and relocate them back into the shelters."

"It's being dubbed Turning the Tide," Joel said. "I'm just not sure which way the tide is turning or who it's turning for."

According to the *Gotham Gazette*, of the ninety or so shelters cited as part of the Turning the Tide program, thirty-one were in the Bronx, fourteen in Manhattan, nineteen in Brooklyn, fourteen in Queens and two on Staten Island.

"I don't know what the answer is," I said. "But there isn't a single person in our crew who is going back into a shelter. We're either going to find single occupancy rooms for them or we're going to have to live with them on our streets."

Jacquelyn Simone, a policy analyst at the Coalition for the Homeless, told *Gotham Gazette* that "It is possible the administration may be on track with the goals they've set. However, it remains to be seen if that capacity will be able to meet the needs in light of the economic devastation brought about by the pandemic."

Andrea Kepler, the former director of a BronxWorks shelter, claimed that moving its residents to the OYO Times Square hotel where each person had their own room with a microwave and small refrigerator was a success. More people obeyed the rules in the hotel than at the shelter because they didn't want to lose their rooms. As Kepler put it, "When you get down to it, it's not science. It's about really doing basic human things that we all want for ourselves."

Joel and I had no answers, but we knew one thing for sure—the shelter system was not the answer for our group of homeless friends. It also did not seem reasonable to house the homeless indefinitely in hotels. The city needed thousands of single occupancy units. There were empty office buildings everywhere I looked. I wondered if maybe some of them would be converted to public housing.

And could we agree to do this?

■ — ■ — ■

MAGGIE WRIGHT, NOVEMBER 2020

It was the first Thanksgiving in four years that I had the ability to cook a meal. Thanksgiving is my favorite holiday, and I wanted to cook more than anything. Traci took me to the grocery store. She bought everything necessary to make a true Thanksgiving feast, right down to the pie. William hadn't had a real home-cooked Thanksgiving dinner in almost twenty years. He cried when I pulled the turkey out of the oven. It was one of the best nights I had in a long time.

In January, Traci left for Turks, and I was heartbroken. I missed my friend and hadn't realized how much I had come to rely on our daily visits. I did my best to keep an eye on everyone while she was gone, and I kept in touch with her via Skype. When they returned to the city, I was thrilled to have her back.

It was around this time that my parents officially decided that they would be moving back to New York. My father was not in good shape. Alzheimer's. The thought of my parents returning to New York was both thrilling and terrifying. I had not seen them since December 2016, and I was a different person than the one they had hugged goodbye at the airport.

The thought of seeing my father in a diminished state terrified me. He helped me when I was on the street. When the weather was bad I would call him up and he would say "Hi Mel. I saw the weather report for New York and knew you would be calling. I'll send you some money for a hotel." Picturing him with a cane, not knowing what was going on, was traumatizing. I didn't want to see it.

I think that is why the thought of obtaining my driver's permit was so daunting. My mother was insistent that I get it so I could help her take my father to his numerous doctor appointments. I was torn. While I desperately wanted to help in any way I could, the thought of that much responsibility overwhelmed me—operating a vehicle, showing up on time to ensure my father was prompt for all his appointments. I didn't know if I could do it.

So I resorted to the one thing I knew best—self sabotage. I made three appointments to take my permit test, and I made an excuse every time. "I didn't study" I told myself. "You're not feeling well enough to take the test today," I told myself the next time. I was good at excuses. I didn't want to admit the truth. I was scared. It took me a while to admit that, and in the process almost destroyed my relationship with my mother for a second time. In the end, with Traci's help, I would gain the confidence to take the test and pass it. It was one of my proudest days in years.

CHAPTER 16

Spring Hope

---◼---

May brought the warm weather but also a devastating loss for Tony, which started, ironically, with the arrival of his much-awaited stimulus check. He celebrated by buying new clothes and a small TV, but unfortunately, also, a large bottle of vodka.

A large bottle of vodka did not mix well with Tony's methadone treatment. He quickly became drunk, loud and belligerent. What might have proved to be a good lesson for Tony turned into a disaster when his behavior attracted the attention of a nearby police officer. Tony's good friend, Orlando, called Joel.

"Tony's just been arrested. It looked to me like he had a seizure when the police cuffed him."

"Where did they take him?"

"I have no idea."

"They'll probably just give him a disorderly conduct ticket and release him," Joel said, in an effort to calm Orlando.

When Tony did not reappear the following week, we grew worried. He'd not been in touch with his case worker, he'd not been to work at the bodega, and he hadn't even called his girlfriend, Juanita. Of even greater concern was the fact that he'd not been to the Greenwich House, his methadone treatment center, nor to his safe haven room at The Travelers.

"This can only mean bad news," I said to Joel. "Maybe he's in jail somewhere. Let's try calling a bail bondsman."

"Good idea," Joel agreed, and immediately looked up the number. We provided Tony's dates of birth and arrest. Armed with these two pieces of critical information, the woman who answered the phone was able to locate Tony's name in the system.

"Here he is," she said, with a cheerful tone that seemed more appropriate for finding an old friend on Facebook, rather than a person who had been arrested. "But my records show that he was released. As of now, he is not in police custody."

"Well, that's great, but do you know where he is then?" Joel asked.

"I'm sorry, all I can see in my records is that he was arrested, charged with a misdemeanor and released."

Another week elapsed with no word from Tony.

"Do you think he's dead—or even worse?" Joel asked one morning.

"I don't have the feeling he's gone," I replied. "But this is not good."

"Agreed, and there is nothing we can do but wait."

To our delight, Kyle suddenly reappeared. At the end of May both Joel and I received simultaneous, and nearly identical, texts from him late one night.

Hey, it's Kyle. I just wanted you to know that I've been away for the last month, but I'm back now.

I was eager to reply. *Great. I still have your shoes. Do you want them?*

I sure do, Kyle texted back.

We're not in the city now. I'll bring them around on Monday. Hang out on 37th Street.

Okay. I'll be waiting.

Need anything else?

A few tee shirts would be great.

As soon as we returned to the city on Monday morning, I gathered Kyle's things together, made him lunch, and set out. As I turned right on 37th Street, I saw him panhandling at the corner near Madison Avenue. Joyful, I broke into an all-out sprint.

Kyle saw me running, and the look on his face was a mixture of confusion and concern. "Why are you running? I'm right here."

"Where have you been?" I asked in a harsher tone than I intended to use. I'd learned that a harsh tone did not work well when communicating with anyone, least of all, with homeless people. I softened my voice. "Joel and I have been looking for you for the past month. I even went up to Columbus Circle and walked around all day asking every homeless person I saw if they'd seen you."

"Why would you do that?"

"Karen told me she saw you up there."

"Yeah, I was up there for a while. Then I went downtown to the Lincoln Tunnel area to help out one of my friends who'd broken his leg."

"That's so nice of you, but can't you let us know where you are?"

"I don't have any way to do that."

"You texted the other night?"

"I had to trade my dinner just to use that phone to send you those few messages."

"I'll get you another one of those cheap flip phones," I offered.

"Great. Thanks."

"Be around here tomorrow, and Joel will come by and take you to the store to have it set up."

"Yes, Mom."

Kyle gave me a bear hug, looked into my eyes, and said goodbye. I knew I'd not done the right thing by expressing too much concern for him. Kyle was in an advanced state of heroin addiction, and I could tell he was much worse off than the last time I'd seen him. Rail thin to begin with, it seemed as though he'd lost twenty pounds.

Maggie had explained to me, more than once, that it was painful if people showed too much concern for a homeless person. Up to a certain point, it was welcome. But if it seemed like someone cared too much, the attention would have a negative impact because a heightened degree of responsibility came with having people in your life who cared. I tried to walk the tightrope as best as I could with all of them, but it was difficult to not slip off of it sometimes with Maggie and Kyle, especially. I loved them. Plain and simple.

The following day, Joel walked up and down 37th Street looking for Kyle.

No Kyle sighting.

Two weeks later, still no Kyle.

"Great," I complained one night. "Now both Tony and Kyle are missing."

Joel pointed out the obvious.

"If Kyle wants you to find him, he knows how."

By June, New Yorkers were coming back to work in larger numbers and traffic noticeably increased. The virus was on the decline across the entire state, and the number of vaccinated people was rising. Commuters returning to the city through Penn Station were especially surprised to see how much the city had changed during the year and three months they'd been working remotely. The homeless population on the West Side, especially in the Hell's Kitchen neighborhood, had skyrocketed after hundreds of homeless people in shelters had been moved into nearby hotels. Most of the sheltered residents were inconspicuous, but a growing number with mental health issues shouted obscenities as they roamed the streets, urinated on the sidewalks, and otherwise created an inhospitable environment for residents and commuters.

The complaints grew louder and the housing debate escalated with avid proponents for change on both sides of the issue. Many commuters expressed fear; others expressed concern. Most people, however, agreed on one thing—the number of homeless people on the streets had sky-rocketed since the pandemic began in March of 2020.

Giselle Routhier, policy director for the Coalition for the Homeless, blamed the state for not providing enough mental health services and single occupancy rooms. Her plea was passionate and bold. "What we actually need for the city to do is to offer folks on the streets access to single occupancy rooms where they can come inside and feel that they are safe from the elements and from the spread of the coronavirus."

In May, Mayor de Blasio had announced that he planned to build a homeless shelter on Billionaire's Row, an elite neighborhood near the luxurious Plaza Hotel. The area boasts some of the most expensive homes in the United States, including a penthouse that sold for $238 million in 2019.

Businesses and residents protested. Lawsuits were filed. At the end of May, a judge in New York's Court of Appeals had ruled that the plans to convert the closed Park Savoy Hotel into a homeless shelter could proceed, and the following year, its first residents moved in.

On June 15th, Governor Cuomo announced that New York State had achieved a seventy percent vaccination rate, and fireworks erupted throughout the state. Within the hour of Governor Cuomo's announcement, Mayor de Blasio made one of his own, stating that the 8,000 homeless people who were living in hotels would be returned to shelters by the end of July. A series of lawsuits ensued.

Mayor de Blasio attempted to justify his decision. "It is time to move homeless folks who were in hotels for a temporary period of time back to shelters where they can get the support they need." Governor Cuomo expressed his agreement, saying that as long as all shelter residents wore masks, he had no objections. I was flabbergasted. Even the issue of where to house the homeless came down to wearing masks.

"This is just one more reason they won't return to the shelter," I said to Joel.

"Agreed. But what are the options?"

The New York Times summed up what appeared to be an intractable dilemma. "The announcement signals the beginning of the end to a living arrangement that was popular with many homeless people, many of whom said that a private hotel room provided a vastly better living experience than sleeping in a shelter. Some said they would sooner live in the street than go back to a group shelter, where many residents are battling mental illness or substance abuse or both."

Bob, whose health continued to decline, finally agreed to move into an assisted living facility after securing a promise from his case worker that he would be allowed to return to the now non-existent telephone booth during the day, his health permitting. Joel praised him for finally making the decision.

"It's the best option for you. Your health continues to decline and you really can't take care of yourself properly."

"I know. But I ain't happy about going into some old people's home. Even my mother lives in her own place."

"Yes, but your mother hasn't been living on the streets for the last ten years, so she's in much better shape than you are, despite your age difference."

"And what about Cathy? Who's going to look after her?" Bob asked.

"We're here, and you know Cathy is capable of taking care of herself."

"She'll be back on these streets if they kick us out of the Y."

"Her case worker will make sure she gets placed in a room," Joel promised.

'I'm not so sure about that," Bob said and frowned.

"You made the right decision," Joel assured him again. "It's time that you took care of yourself."

"I guess you're right. I sure don't want to end up missing like poor Tony. At least if I die, someone will let my mother know."

We did everything we could to find Tony, including filing a missing person's report. Maggie canvassed every known place he'd ever been seen in the city. No one knew where he was. I still didn't *feel* like Tony was dead, but logic dictated that my feeling must be wrong. We were preparing ourselves to accept the inevitable.

Then the phone rang.

It was Tony's girlfriend, Juanita. "Tony's in the hospital on the Upper West Side."

"He's alive?" Joel asked, shocked.

"Barely. He's on life support."

"How did you find out?"

"The nurse saw the name of his case worker in his wallet and called her. She called Orlando, and he called me. Tony's in the ICU. I'm on my way up to the hospital now."

Two hours later, Juanita called again. "I'm here with Tony. He's not in good shape. They want to take him off life support. But they need a family member to sign the papers."

"I don't think he has any family left," Joel said. "Or if he does, we don't know of anyone."

"Just as well, if you ask me," replied Juanita. "I just saw his leg move."

Over the next week, Juanita and Orlando visited Tony every day and called us every night with the report. Nothing much had changed since the day Juanita saw Tony's leg move. The plans to remove him from his breathing tube appeared to be moving forward, despite the lack of a family member available to sign the papers.

Joel and I debated going to the hospital to say goodbye but decided it would be too painful to see Tony on life support and, in any event, there was nothing we could do. However, on July 2nd, I woke up early and decided to go anyway. Two buses later, I arrived in the lobby of the hospital. The check-in line snaked out the door to the sidewalk. Nevertheless, I decided I might as well wait since I was there. An hour later, I walked into the ICU, turned right towards the nurses' station and practically walked directly into Tony's room. I steadied my nerves, sure that what I was about to see would be upsetting.

Then the miracle happened.

Tony was awake and sitting up in a chair beside his bed. A nurse was by his side. At first, all I could do was point at Tony. Finally, my mouth moved.

"He's awake?" I asked in disbelief.

"Woke up this morning," she replied with a big smile.

Tony recognized me at once, despite my face being covered by a mask. At this point, the hospitals were among the few remaining places in the city where masks were still mandatory.

The breathing device in Tony's neck prevented any sound from coming out of his mouth when he spoke, but the nurse remedied that by inserting a little stopper into the opening. "Let's put your plug in," she announced.

"Hey there, Traci, how you doing?" Tony said, his voice trembling.

"I'm doing pretty well now that I'm seeing you're okay! You had us all scared for the last month."

"I had a seizure."

"Yes, I know."

"They told me I'm going to be in here for six more months."

"Are they treating you well?"

"Yes," Tony replied and began to cry.

I took a video of Tony saying, "Happy Friday," which I texted to Maggie, Joel, Bob, Cathy, Juanita, and Orlando. I then sent it to his case worker and her supervisor, hoping they would realize Tony might be released soon and would need to be immediately placed in a new safe haven room. He'd already lost his room at The Travelers, having not used it for the last month.

The following week, Joel visited Tony, who had been moved to a regular room and, to Joel's astonishment, was talking about being released. Two days later, against medical advice, Tony checked himself out of the hospital, significantly better, but still very disoriented. Amid a torrential downpour and wearing a soaking wet tee-shirt three sizes too big, hospital pajama bottoms, and no shoes, Tony headed directly to the corner where Bob and Cathy sat. Bob asked a nearby building super for a dry shirt, which the super produced.

Tony's case worker moved mountains and found him a new safe haven room the following week. We all breathed a sigh of relief. Tony was in no shape to be roaming the streets, much less sleeping on them.

Much to our surprise and delight, Tony was placed in a safe haven room at the Seafarers International House, now a transitional single room occupancy shelter, located in an ideal location—15th and Third Avenue. A further blessing was that Tony's steadfast friend, Orlando, who'd been homeless for twenty-two years, was also given a room there! Of all the homeless people we'd met, Orlando was the only one who did not drink or use drugs.

In sharp contrast to the hardships being faced by some of our homeless friends, our wealthy friends were celebrating the continuous rise in the stock market. The economy was improving. For the well-to-do, anyway. *The New York Times* highlighted the reality that only the rich were benefitting from the economic recovery in an opinion piece by Karen Petrou published on July 12th. According to the article, by the beginning of 2021, the richest one percent of Americans held nearly a third of the nation's wealth. The bottom half held just two percent despite the fact that these new records were set following a year of stimulus checks, unemployment benefits, and low interest rates.

I woke up one morning and decided to head uptown again to look for Kyle, even though I knew it was unlikely that I'd find him. Two hours later, I gave up my effort, boarded the next bus down Fifth Avenue and got off at 38th Street. Without even thinking about where I was going, I found myself walking south one block to 37th Street in the hope that I might find Kyle. I walked up and down the street several times. I finally gave up and headed for home, remembering Karen's words. Ironically, Kyle knew how to find me much better than I knew how to locate him.

In late September, Kyle did find me, if only for one day. Walking home from lunch, I noticed a roofless, cardboard hut on my street corner. I stopped to see if anyone was inside, and to my shock, it was Kyle. Sadly, he was so completely unresponsive to my calling out his name that, for a moment, I thought he was dead. Then I noticed a fragile breathing.

I returned to the apartment, made three sandwiches, gathered a few tee-shirts from our stash, and a winter coat Joel had just bought for him at the Good Will. Joel and I went back and stood over his crumpled body, gently repeating his name. Kyle eventually stirred, although he was unable to even sit up. But he recognized us. Of that, at least, I was certain.

"You don't have to get up, Kyle" I said, in a gentle tone. "We've just brought you some sandwiches, shirts and a new winter coat. The nights are getting cool again." Kyle smiled slightly and reached up for our offerings, as I leaned over his cardboard construction.

"We love you," Joel said.

"We love you," I added. Kyle did not reply. I noticed a sad grimace on his lifeless face.

Joel and I walked away, arm in arm. I knew I'd never see Kyle again. Or maybe it's more accurate to say that I *believed* I'd never see him again, even if I did leave one, small, hidden place in my heart where I buried the hope I was wrong.

Maggie's parents had relocated to New York, and she was anxious to see them again. It had been almost five years, and she was nervous. Her mother insisted that Maggie get vaccinated—and provide proof—before she would allow her to visit. Maggie complied with her mother's demand, and I was glad. On a micro level, I no longer had to worry about Maggie becoming seriously ill from the virus. On a macro level, one more person was taken out of the path of the delta variant, which was now raging out of control.

Two weeks later, fully vaccinated, Maggie enjoyed a heartfelt and healing reunion with her parents. Some things about Maggie were a surprise to her mother, most notably how much Maggie seem to have aged since their last visit. I'd even noticed Maggie's aging, despite knowing her only eighteen months. Living on the streets is hard, and quite literally, sucks the life out of most people.

"Maggie looks so much older than the last time I saw her," her mother said.

"Imagine what she's been through in the three years that she's lived on the corner of Park Avenue and 30th Street," I replied

"I try not to," her mother said.

Maggie continued to look for a job, applying to every bookstore, coffee shop and clothing store that would accept her application. She got a few interviews but no job offers. Despite being sheltered, it was still obvious Maggie was homeless.

In my heart of hearts, I knew Maggie didn't really want a job. Actually, I believe she wanted one—she just couldn't meet the demands of one. It would be another year before Maggie finally found employment at a major department store. Even before she could go on the initial interview, she needed a haircut and a something appropriate to wear. It was then that I realized just how hard it was to get a job for the homeless.

I felt ashamed for suggesting to more than one homeless person in the previous year that they should "just get a job." I now understood how ridiculous that suggestion was. I'd come a long way in my understanding of what happens to homeless people, especially to those who drop out of the shelter system and end up on the streets. Somehow the sidewalks swallow them up.

Maybe that's because they don't want to be seen.

Maybe it's because it's just too painful for us to see them.

As I fell asleep that night, relieved that Maggie's reunion with her parents had gone well, I pondered the homeless dilemma and realized that I, like so many others, did not have any answers. It did not seem fair to force the hotels to remain as homeless shelters against their will. It also did not seem right, or even possible, to leave the homeless to fend for themselves on the streets. I was both happy and sad that their presence on the sidewalks had finally become a point of public contention. They could no longer be ignored. If only there were more communities like the one that Anne Stembler, CEO of Hand in Hand of Glynn, was building, I thought.

I'm often asked two questions. What can the average person do to help and why did we do this? My advice is simple. If you live in an area where you encounter homeless people, make one sandwich every morning and give it to one person—perhaps on your way to work, or maybe as you drop off your child/children at school. Just one sandwich given to one homeless person. If even one percent of us did that, there would be no more hungry people living on the streets. And these men and women would know that someone, maybe just one person, cared enough about them that day to make a sandwich. As Brian Ourien, Director, Brand Marketing and Communications of the Bowery Mission recently told *AM Metro New York* news, "And so we need a myriad of voices speaking to this from politics to corporate to individuals like you and I to step into this space and think how can I participate in changing the landscape of homelessness in New York City."

And why did Joel and I do this? It might be nice to pretend that we are just the type of people who spend our extra time helping those less fortunate. But that would be a lie. The truth is we simply felt we had no choice but to help.

In the early days of the pandemic, the homeless people in our neighborhood were starving. There is a certain smell to hunger. It's more than the bad breath of an empty stomach. It's ineffable but very real. We felt it was impossible for us to stay safely sheltered in our apartment while they were in daily view from our windows and do nothing. We knew the risks, and we were scared. Nevertheless, we believed we'd be protected. At some point during our efforts, we came to understand a vital truth that had eluded us up until that moment.

In getting to know these homeless people we learned that the *truth*—ours and theirs—was not fixed. It mutated, dependent on the timing, the teller and the perceiver. But an even more valuable insight was that truth, like the virus, was relentless in its battle for survival, jabbing and crawling its way into the light.

Joel and I are not the same people we were before the virus claimed 2020 as its victim. No one is the same—the city has changed and so have its residents. Despite the deaths, despite the fear, there was always something that followed us through the streets of Manhattan on the darkest of days. It's difficult to name, although it was a palpable force. It felt warm and comforting, like a roaring fire on a cold winter night. Maybe it was a deep sense of hope that blazed its way up through the cracks in the sidewalks and seeped into our hearts, unbidden, but welcome.

■ – ■ – ■

MAGGIE WRIGHT, OCTOBER 2021

The time was rapidly drawing closer to the reunion with my parents. I was more nervous than I thought I would be. When my mother demanded I be vaccinated, I was relieved to have an additional two weeks to prepare.

Our reunion went better than I could have imagined. While I had been so nervous before getting there, the nerves dissipated as soon as I entered their home—these were my parents. I had missed them! My father beamed when he saw me. He was genuinely happy to be in my presence, which warmed my soul. Even my mother, who was usually not one to show emotion, hugged me tightly. She, too, seemed genuinely happy to see me.

Of course, nothing is all sunshine and rainbows. I could tell she was surprised at my appearance and asked me about it. She commented on my weight loss. After all, I was now over a hundred pounds lighter than when she'd last seen me. And although my hair was newly cut and colored, she commented about how old I looked, saying I had aged a lifetime since we'd last seen one another. There were a million things I wanted to say about that issue but chose to stay quiet. There were some things better left unsaid.

I left their home with a spring in my step and dove headfirst into a search for a job even though I was absolutely terrified at the prospect. I was slowly reclaiming my identity, but a job was a huge undertaking for me, for many reasons.

It had been a long time since I'd worked a regular job. Not only did that cause a huge gap in my resume, but my brain was so far removed from the prospect of "working" that it seemed an impossible task. I had not managed to maintain a schedule of any kind since 2017. How could I possibly work any type of normal shift?

Of course, there were a few other scattered problems. I had a layer of dirt on my hands, and under my fingernails, which I was pretty sure would never go away. I was missing some teeth. I'd lost my glasses years before and was virtually blind without them. I had no wardrobe, no resume, no prospects, and no hope. All I knew was I needed a job. Desperately.

I was terrified at the thought of being rejected and didn't even know where to start to fix all the problems that stood in my way. One morning, I woke up hungry, broke, and miserable at the thought of struggling to make it through another day. I decided I had to swallow my pride, get over my fears, and start the process of finding a job.

When I broached the subject with Traci, she was thrilled. I sent her my old resume, which she promptly fixed up. When she sent it back to me I was so excited—it looked professional, and she had even included a picture of me on it. The smiling face looking back at me seemed unrecognizable. If only the people who would receive this resume knew what I had been through!

I went to the store and printed out twenty-five copies. I was so excited I even gave one to the manager there—I could do this. Now, I had to work on the physical barriers that might prevent me from working. That was pretty hard on me to take stock of, as I looked in the mirror at the face staring back at me. The streets had aged me more than I had realized.

Traci took me to get a pair of glasses. As I was trying on frames, I couldn't believe that I was going to get my sight back. Having poor vision for so long had been a challenge. I had become resigned to the fact that I couldn't see. I counted the days until the glasses were ready, and when I put them on for the first time, I cried for ten minutes.

Once I had glasses, Traci took me to get my hair done. I left the salon looking like a real person again. My nails were cleaned, trimmed, and painted a bright red, almost screaming for them to be seen. Traci had helped me get this far. Now, it was my turn to do the rest.

I applied for every job I could find. I walked into bookstores and restaurants and put in every application I could online. When I got a call back from a large department store, I was ecstatic. I had applied to be a merchandise assistant, but they were calling me for an executive assistant position!

When I told Traci she was so excited she took me shopping for an interview outfit. We picked out a beautiful jacket and slacks. The outfit was perfect and gave me the confidence I needed.

As I got dressed for my interview, I was shaking. As I slipped on my shoes and looked in the mirror, I was astonished at the woman I saw standing before me. I had come so far in my quest to reclaim the person I knew I could be. I was ready for this. I walked out of the house confident I would get the job.

And I did!

EPILOGUE

Most of our homeless friends are still sheltered. Donations of coats, sweaters and money continue to arrive and are in turn distributed to other homeless people. Many mornings, I hear Joel announce, "Joel's haberdashery is now open." As he heads out the door, laden with the day's donations made possible through the generosity of so many others, I feel grateful that the pandemic led us to the streets and into the lives of our homeless friends.

Maggie and I remain friends. She is on good terms with her parents and in a healthy relationship with William. They recently adopted a little dog they adore—a puppy given up by her owners during the pandemic because they could not afford to feed her. Maggie is back in college finishing her undergraduate degree.

Kyle is still missing. We have not seen him since that day in September. My heart is broken. I often think about all the mothers who have lost a child to addiction. I wonder every day whether I pushed Kyle too hard and too often to get treatment. I remain hopeful that one day he will show back up on 37th Street. I still feel like his aunt, if not, his mother. While "losing" Kyle has been difficult, it has made me more aware of my many blessings.

Tony is doing well. He returned to his job at the bodega even though he no longer needs free food, as he is given three meals a day at his safe haven house. He takes the free meals, however, and shares the food with other homeless people who are still unsheltered.

Rick maintains a relationship with his mother. A homeless man recently attacked him with a pipe. Maggie was upset but saw the karma in it. Maggie knows where to find him but stays away, much to William's delight, her mother's, and ours.

Henry is still in his safe haven room and keeping his parole appointments—a four month stint in prison reminds him to set his alarm clock when he has an appointment the following day.

Unfortunately, Mark is back out on the street. Recently, he showed up on our block. He was not in good shape.

Bob is still at the YMCA, awaiting his room in assisted living. He sits on the corner every day with Cathy. His health is poor but stable. Cathy told us that her recent liver screen showed no signs of damage from the Hep-C. She has assumed the role of keeping an eye on Bob, instead of the other way around. She's quick to tattle on him when his drinking gets out of hand, which unfortunately, is often.

Mr. Banks, the well-dressed gentleman we met before Easter, was recently housed after finally admitting to himself, as well as to Joel, that he was indeed homeless. He still roams Park Avenue during the day, looking even more dapper now that he is sheltered and clean. The last time we saw him he told us that he went to Yale Law School. I didn't have the heart to remind him that he'd once told us he graduated from Fordham.

Tammy and Ed are still missing. We hope this means they were given another chance and are safely sheltered somewhere in a different part of the city.

And as for what happened to Shawn, the young Black man who ran down the street after us hoping to get a sandwich, Maggie recently told me the truth about his sudden disappearance. He was a member of one of the most notorious gangs in the country but posing as a member of its rival. When his true identity was discovered, he literally started running down Park Avenue, Forrest Gump style, and has not been seen or heard from since.

Sometimes we are asked a third question in addition to the two mentioned above. What did we do for our group of homeless friends that society, the homeless agencies, and the other pedestrians who dropped money into their tattered cups didn't do that made the difference in our relationships with them? The answer may seem trite to some, but it's true.

We loved them.

■ – ■ – ■

MAGGIE WRIGHT, OCTOBER 2021

I didn't tell anyone I was coming. At seven o'clock in the morning, I boarded the bus, shaking. As we got closer to Atlantic City, my heart started to pound and my mouth became extremely dry. I don't think I had ever been more nervous in my entire life.

We pulled into Atlantic City, and I went to the gas station where I purchased a pack of cigarettes and bottle of soda. As I waited for the Uber to take me to the field where my son would be playing football and my daughter cheering I could hear my heart thumping in my chest. I smoked three cigarettes before the car pulled up in front of me.

As we drove to the field I looked at the familiar sights and marveled at how long it had been since I had been in New Jersey and how different I was since the last time I'd been there. It might as well have been a lifetime ago since I had driven down those streets and made those right turns on red lights.

As we pulled up to the field I saw one of my old neighbors. "What are you doing here? Your son cannot see you," he shouted.

The last thing I wanted to do was upset my son before his football game. I walked around the block to smoke a cigarette and figure out what to do next.

I had come too far to turn back now. As I returned to the field, I saw my mother-in-law. We agreed that I could stand on the visitor's sideline to watch the game, after which she would speak with me about seeing the children. I thanked her and turned to go.

As I was walking away she yelled after me, "What happened to the rest of you?" It took every ounce of strength I possessed not to respond that my body had rotted away on the sidewalk during the last three years.

As I stood on the sidelines watching my son, my heart swelled with pride. Even though he didn't know it yet, I was there. I had finally made it back to New Jersey, back to my children. My eyes teared up as I watched him on that field. I couldn't believe I was looking at him in real life. Just then, I heard the sweetest words I have ever heard in my life.

"Mommy? I knew that was you!"

My daughter was running towards me. She had spotted me when she entered the field and thought she was dreaming. As I wrapped my arms around her, I couldn't hold back the tears. I was finally hugging my child again. We spent some time together before she ran back off to be with her friends, making me promise I would stay to see her halftime cheer routine. I promised her I would, and I did.

That day changed everything for me. The hardest part of being homeless was being separated from my children. On my darkest days and longest nights, I feared that I would never see them again. For the first time since becoming homeless, I felt like I was through the worst of my self-inflicted storm and that there was light ahead. I had been chasing that light for a long time.

That was the first day I saw it.

My story is filled with terrible choices, broken promises, and shattered dreams. It is also the tale of triumph in the face of adversity, the return of peace to my soul, and an unearned grace that I am anxious to share with others.

Faith is twenty-four hours of doubt and one minute of hope.

--*THE INNOCENTS,* **2006** FILM

About the Author

Traci Medford-Rosow is the *USA Today* bestselling author of two books. The first, *Inflection Point: War and Sacrifice in Corporate America*, was published by Pegasus Books in 2015. The second, *Unblinded: One Man's Courageous Journey through Darkness to Sight,* was published by Morgan James in 2018. In addition to being named to *USA Today, Unblinded* is  also a *Publishers Weekly, Indie Bound,* Amazon and Barnes and Noble bestseller. *Unblinded* was named to Kirkus Reviews' Best Books of 2020.

Traci is currently a partner in the New York City law firm Richardson & Rosow. Previously, she worked at Pfizer as Senior VP and Chief Intellectual Property Counsel, Global Head of IP Litigation and General Counsel of Europe. She is the founder of the College Education Milestone Foundation.

Traci has made numerous guest appearances on radio shows, podcasts, and at book signings. She lives in New York City with her husband. They have two adult children.

Contact Traci at www.tracimedfordrosow.com

Appendix A:

Also by Traci Medford-Rosow

Excerpt from *Unblinded*

Chapter 1—Blue Eyes

Kevin couldn't shake an ominous feeling that had been nagging him for two days.

He glanced at the liquor cabinet. It was too early to have a drink, even by his liberal definition of when cocktail hour began.

He distracted himself from that thought by picking up the *New York Times*. And there it was again. The same blurriness he'd experienced two days earlier at work. He was doing some research for his latest grant proposal when he noticed he was unable to read an article he'd pulled off the reference shelf. The words were blurry. Soft. Out of focus.

He hadn't been too concerned about it at the time. He thought he was just tired after a long day at the office, and anyway, it was a problem easily solved. He made the short trip to the Xerox machine and enlarged the print.

But this was Saturday morning in his own home. And he'd had a good night's sleep. His eyes were not in the least strained from a long day at work. Kevin wondered if he needed glasses. He started to blink rapidly, but his efforts produced little, if any, improvement in his vision. He put the newspaper on his coffee table and headed for the bathroom. He washed and dried his face, paying particular attention to his eyes. As he returned to his living room, he glanced out the window. It seemed foggy outside. At the same moment, he heard the weather report on the television—bitterly cold with abundant sunshine.

Kevin couldn't dwell on it for long, however. He was going to visit his parents on Long Island. Walking across town to Penn Station was uneventful. Kevin had done it so many times; the ten blocks from his apartment on Lexington and 37th posed no problem, even though his vision was still blurry.

He didn't need to read the information board—his train always departed from track eighteen. He headed toward it. Once on the train, he sat down in his usual seat next to the window and made himself comfortable. It was a forty-minute trip out to Mineola.

He hadn't brought the newspaper with him. There was no point in reminding himself about the eyesight issue more than necessary. Anyway, he was still convinced it was no big deal. It was, he thought once again, as simple as needing glasses. After all, he was thirty-six, and many of his friends had purchased their first pair a decade earlier.

His mother was sitting in her car when the train pulled into the station. Kevin could always count on her waiting in the parking lot—even on those evenings when he'd fallen asleep on the train and missed his stop.

Ruth Liesenberg Coughlin was a nurturing and devoted mother. She was a private duty nurse by training which suited her personality well. A kind and loving woman, not only to her family but also to her friends, she was adored by everyone. Kevin never failed to be in awe of, or grateful for, her loyalty. On the other hand, Kevin felt that his father, Walter J. Coughlin, an accountant by profession, was somewhat emotionally distant. Nevertheless, Kevin appreciated the fact that he'd been a good provider for his family and a faithful husband to Ruth.

Kevin was the youngest of three children. His sister, Kathy, and brother, John, were ten and eight years older. The gap made him feel like an only child for much of his youth, especially once Kathy and John left for college.

Kevin was overweight from the age of five to fifteen. As a result, he lacked confidence and was socially awkward. He had few, if any, close friends. His primary social interactions resulted from his reluctant participation in Little League and his weekly attendance at mass.

In his sophomore year of high school, Kevin decided to transform himself. He went on a diet consisting of tuna fish and Fresca, started working out, and lost forty pounds. Miraculously, as he lost girth he gained height. He grew four inches taller.

Kevin, the short and chubby one, had disappeared along with the fat boy clothes his mother bought for him in the Husky Shop at Sears. Fashionable Levi's and Lacoste polo shirts took their place. He became a tall, slender, green-eyed hunk just in time for college.

Kevin and his mother returned to the family home—the same blue Cape Cod house where he'd grown up. He always loved the back yard; it was one of the deepest and flattest in the neighborhood. It had been a great place for parties in high school. After years of feeling unaccepted, Kevin had gained a modicum of respect from his peers by junior year, even though he suspected it was primarily because of the party venue he was able to provide.

His parents' bedroom was on the first floor; the kids' rooms were upstairs. This provided a fair measure of privacy, which came in handy when Kevin wanted to crank up his radio or record player and listen to his favorite Elton John and Billy Joel albums.

Their neighborhood, like many others on Long Island that were part of the post-war building boom, was built on an old potato field. There were three models to choose from—a Cape Cod, split level, or ranch. This was a big deal in the 1950's. Most of the other neighborhoods in the area had only one choice.

After a quick bite to eat, Kevin set off for Waldbaum's to do his parents' weekly grocery shopping, a chore he had taken over after his father's stroke five years earlier. Kevin stuffed his mother's list into his pocket, and, as usual, assured her he'd be back soon. He always looked forward to his trips to Waldbaum's. In contrast to the city's grocery stores, Waldbaum's was clean and bright. The food was organized, making his task an easy and pleasant one. He knew where to go for the usual items: fruit, vegetables, meat, milk, and the two 12-packs of diet soda his father loved.

That day, however, the store seemed to lack its customary brightness. The colors appeared as muted shades of gray that matched the mood of the winter day. The oranges, lemons and selection of colorful vegetables that filled meticulously arranged display stands looked washed out.

In this dull light, Kevin had a problem reading the grocery list. He stood in the produce department studying it for several minutes, willing the words to come into focus. Short of asking someone in the store to walk around with him like a personal shopper, he knew there was only one thing to do. He would have to return home to ask his mother to read the list aloud to him or write it larger.

Kevin was not eager to do this as he knew it would alarm her. His own internal warning lights were flashing in his head, yet he continued to subdue them with his self-diagnosis that he needed nothing more than a pair of reading glasses.

As he predicted, when Kevin walked in the front door empty-handed, his mother's tone of voice confirmed that she was worried.

"What are you doing back so soon? Where are the groceries?"

"I'm sorry, but I can't read the grocery list, mom. Can you please rewrite it and make it bigger?"

Ruth let out a sound that was somewhat of a grunt mixed with concern and disappeared into the kitchen for another piece of scrap paper. Kevin followed her.

As he sat at the kitchen table waiting for his mother to rewrite the list, he realized that he couldn't see the color of his mother's vivid blue eyes. Or the details of her face, which was remarkably unlined for someone in her seventies.

Kevin didn't say anything. He didn't want to alarm her further. He took the rewritten grocery list from his mother's outstretched hand and glanced at it. He still couldn't make out the words. Reluctant to cause additional worry but unable to return to Waldbaum's with the proffered list, he asked again.

"Mom, would you please make the words a bit bigger? I guess I'm tired from being out late last night, and I'm still having a hard time reading the list."

Kevin hadn't been out late the night before—in fact he hadn't been out at all. Ruth was no longer able to hide her growing concern.

"You need to see an eye doctor first thing next week," she said adamantly. "Please promise me you'll make an appointment when you get back to the city."

Kevin nodded his agreement. He then cast his eyes over the new grocery list with its oversized letters written in black felt-tipped pen on a yellow legal pad. His mother gave him an anxious look. He simply touched her shoulder and headed back to Waldbaum's to complete his shopping.

Kevin didn't discuss his eyesight with his father that day, but he overheard his mother talking to him.

"Walter, Kevin is having problems with his eyesight, and I'm worried."

Kevin walked out of earshot of the conversation. He didn't want to hear the rest. Kevin could no longer convince himself, much less his parents, that his poor eyesight could be corrected with a pair of reading glasses.

By the time Kevin returned to his apartment that evening, he knew something was very wrong. It was as if the lights were being dimmed. If he couldn't understand what was going on, he could at least numb it.

He reached for the vodka.

He poured himself a full glass leaving only enough room for a splash of cranberry juice. He paused when he took the container from the fridge.

Something was strange.

He picked up a carton of orange juice. He blinked rapidly, shook his head, and looked once more at the drink containers, comparing them side-by-side. He shook his head, blinked again and rubbed his eyes.

Kevin was no longer able to see colors.

A free ebook edition is available with the purchase of this book.

To claim your free ebook edition:

1. Visit MorganJamesBOGO.com
2. Sign your name CLEARLY in the space
3. Complete the form and submit a photo of the entire copyright page
4. You or your friend can download the ebook to your preferred device

A **FREE** ebook edition is available for you or a friend with the purchase of this print book.

CLEARLY SIGN YOUR NAME ABOVE

Instructions to claim your free ebook edition:
1. Visit MorganJamesBOGO.com
2. Sign your name CLEARLY in the space above
3. Complete the form and submit a photo of this entire page
4. You or your friend can download the ebook to your preferred device

Print & Digital Together Forever.

Snap a photo

Free ebook

Read anywhere